To: Liz
May You
Follow Your Passi[on]

Love,
Maggie

MASAI
MYTHS, TALES
AND RIDDLES

MASAI
MYTHS, TALES AND RIDDLES

A. C. HOLLIS

DOVER PUBLICATIONS, INC.
MINEOLA, NEW YORK

Bibliographical Note

This Dover edition, first published in 2003, is a new selection from *The Masai: Their Language and Folklore,* published by Oxford, at the Clarendon Press, London, in 1905. We have left out the Masai-language samples, have Americanized the English, have slightly reworded two of the proverbs to make them understandable, and have translated into English one passage the author wrote in Latin.

Library of Congress Cataloging-in-Publication Data

Hollis, Alfred Claud, Sir, 1874–
    [Masai. Selections.]
    Masai myths, tales, and riddles / A.C. Hollis.
       p. cm.
    "A new selection from The Masai; their language and folklore, published by Oxford, at the Clarendon Press, London, in 1905"-T.p. verso.
    ISBN 0-486-43199-1 (pbk.)
    1. Masai language. 2. Masai (African people)—Folklore. 3. Mythology, Masai. I. Title.

PR8501.H62 2003
496'.5—dc21   2003055306

Manufactured in the United States of America
Dover Publications, Inc., 31 East 2nd Street, Mineola, N.Y. 11501

Contents

Contents   v

STORIES

The Hare and the Elephants

A HARE THAT lived near a river one day saw some elephants going to the kraals of their fathers-in-law. He said to the biggest one, who was carrying a bag of honey: "Father, ferry me across, for I am a poor person."

The elephant told him to get on his back, and when he had climbed up, they started.

While they were crossing the river, the hare ate the honey, and as he was eating it, he let some of the juice fall onto the elephant's back. On being asked what he was dropping, he replied that he was weeping, and that it was the tears of a poor child that were falling. When they reached the opposite bank, the hare asked the elephants to give him some stones to throw at the birds.

He was given some stones, and he put them into the honey bag. He then asked to be set down, and as soon as he was on the ground again he told the elephants to be off.

They continued their journey until they reached the kraal of the big one's father-in-law, where they opened the honey bag. When they found that the stones had been substituted for the honey, they jumped up and returned to search for the hare, whom they found feeding. As they approached, however, the hare saw them, and entered a hole. The elephants followed him, and the biggest one thrust his trunk into the hole, and seized him by the leg, whereupon the hare said: "I think you have caught hold of a root." On hearing this the elephant let go his leg and seized a root. The hare then cried out: "You have broken me, you have broken me," which made the elephant pull all the harder until at length he became tired.

While the elephant was pulling at the root, the hare slipped

1

out of the hole and ran away. As he ran, he met some baboons, and called out to them to help him. They inquired why he was running so fast, and he replied that he was being chased by a great big person. The baboons told him to go and sit down, and promised not to give him up. The hare entered the baboons' lair while they sat down outside and waited. Presently the elephant arrived, and asked if the hare had passed that way. The baboons inquired whether he would give them anything if they pointed out the hare's hiding place. The elephant said he would give them whatever they asked for, and when they said they wanted a cup full of his blood, he consented to give it to them, after satisfying himself that the cup was small. The baboons then shot an arrow into his neck, and the blood gushed forth.

After the elephant had lost a considerable quantity of blood, he inquired if the cup was not full. But the baboons had made a hole in the bottom, and when the elephant looked at it, he saw that it was still half empty. The baboons jeered at him, and said he had no courage, so he told them to fill the cup.

They continued to bleed him, but still the cup would not fill, and at length he sank exhausted to the ground and died.

The hare having nothing more to fear was then able to leave his hiding place.

The Warriors and the Devil

Two young brothers once lived together with their parents. In course of time they grew up, were circumcised, and became warriors.

One day their father gave them a bullock, and told them to go and slaughter it; but they decided that they could only slaughter it in a place where there was no man, or animal, or bird, or insect, or anything living. They therefore took their spears, shields, swords, and clubs, and went to look for such a place.

After searching unsuccessfully for five months they entered a big forest where there was no living creature. They waited for a few days, and then, as they could not find anything that had life, they built a slaughterhouse, and slaughtered their bullock.

After they had killed the animal, the elder one gave his

brother the stomach, and told him to go and draw some water. The younger one went to the river, but when he drew the water, it cried out: "He has drawn me, he has drawn me." He was much frightened and ran away, and as he ran, the forest laughed. He related what had occurred to his brother, who told him to spit as he was a coward. The elder one took the stomach of the ox himself, and went to the river, when the water called out as before: "He has drawn me, he has drawn me." He replied: "Yes, I have drawn you on purpose," and took the water back with him.

The younger brother was then sent to cut wood, but when he took hold of the tree, the firewood cried out: "He has broken me, he has broken me." Again much alarmed, he returned to the slaughterhouse, and told his brother that the firewood had rebuked him. His brother did the same as on the other occasion: he called the younger warrior a coward, and told him to spit; he then took his sword, and went to cut the firewood. The firewood cried out when he cut it, but the warrior replied that he was cutting it on purpose, and took it back with him.

On his arrival he told his brother to go and cut some skewers. When he cut them, however, the skewers cried out: "He has cut us, he has cut us." He left them and ran back to the kraal to tell his brother, who again called him a coward, and told him to spit, while he went himself to cut the skewers. The same thing happened as before. The skewers cried out on being cut, but the warrior told them he had done it on purpose, and returned with them to the slaughterhouse.

The warriors then roasted some meat and had a meal, after which they went to sleep.

During the night a devil came and put out their fire. He then lit his eye, which resembled a fire, and lay down. Later on the elder warrior woke up his brother, and told him to make up the fire. The younger one got up and seized the devil's eye, thinking it was a brand. The devil thereupon swallowed him, and went away, while the elder warrior cried after him: "Go now, but tomorrow I will look for you."

At dawn he started off in pursuit, and when he found the devil, he noticed that he had nine heads and a very big toe.

The devil told the warrior to go away, and said he did not wish to hurt him as he was brave. The warrior refused, however, and told the devil he wanted to fight. The devil rushed at him, and tried to kick him, but the warrior caught the kick on his shield, and cut off one of his adversary's heads. The devil then fled, and the warrior called out to him that he would return on the morrow, after which he went back to the slaughterhouse, and rested.

The next day he followed up the devil, and in the fight which ensued cut off another head. The devil ran away again, and the warrior told him that he would return the following morning to kill him.

When he came to the spot the next day, he found the devil very weak from losing two of his heads, and he easily dispatched him, after which he cut off the big toe. Every kind of animal came out from the toe, and last of all came the warrior's brother.

The two returned to their slaughterhouse and rested for three days, at the end of which the younger warrior asked his brother to take him home, as he was afraid to remain there any longer.

The Warrior and His Sisters, or Why Free Love Is Permitted Among the Masai

There once lived an old man who had two daughters and a son. In course of time the children grew up, and the boy became a warrior. War then broke out between the old man's people and a neighboring tribe, with the result that the former feared to take their cattle to the salt lick, as they were accustomed to do once or twice a month. The cattle suffered in consequence, and gave no milk.

When the old man's son saw that his cattle were falling ill, he made up his mind to take them to the salt lick, and to die with them if necessary. His elder sister accompanied him, and as he was leaving the paternal roof, he told his younger sister that if she saw smoke issuing from the watering place, she might know that he was safe.

On his arrival at the salt lick he erected his kraal, and encircled it with a hedge of thorns. The next morning he took his cattle out to graze, leaving his sister to look after the kraal. For some days the enemy did not come near them, but one morning they suddenly appeared. The girl was alone at the time, and they made love to her, after which they departed.

On the warrior's return in the evening he noticed the footmarks, but said nothing to his sister. The next morning he drove his cattle out to graze as usual, and when he had taken them to a safe distance, he returned and hid himself near the kraal. The enemy came again and made love to the girl. When they were about to leave, the warrior heard his sister say to them: "If you come this evening, I will sing when my brother milks the big cow. You can then take me away and the cattle too."

The warrior went back to his cattle, and in the evening, when he had returned to the kraal, he placed his weapons in readiness, and pretended to milk the big cow. His sister at once commenced to sing, so he left the cow, and seized his weapons. Almost at the same time one of the enemy jumped over the thorn hedge only to be killed by the warrior. Five others met with the same fate, and the remainder fled. The warrior then sallied forth, and collected a lot of firewood with which he lit a fire and burnt the bodies.

It had been raining, and the women of the old man's kraal were repairing the damage done to their huts by plastering them with a mixture of cow dung and clay. The warrior's younger sister was on the roof of the hut, and when she saw the smoke issuing from the salt lick, she cried out: "My brother is safe." She was asked how she knew, and she told everybody what her brother had said to her when he left them.

The next morning all the people of the old man's kraal moved to the salt lick, and their cattle speedily recovered. The warrior related what his sister had done, and her father sought out a man to marry her.

Before this event it was not customary for the young girls to go to the warriors' kraals, and they remained at home till they were married; but when the story of the girl's treachery was known, it was considered safer to let them go, and sing, and dance, and live with the warriors. And this custom has been observed ever since.

The Devil Called Sae-Kidongoi[1]
and the Children

There was once upon a time an old man who had two wives. One of his wives gave birth to a son and a daughter, and then died, leaving her little children to be looked after by their stepmother. But both their stepmother and their father disliked them and treated them badly.

One day the inhabitants of the kraal moved with their cattle to another grazing ground. The two children, however, remained behind in the deserted huts to see if they could pick up any food which might have been left there. They stayed all night, and started off the next morning to follow the cattle trail. But on the road they crossed another trail, that of the devil called Sae-Kidongoi, and they followed this one by mistake, arriving eventually at the devil's kraal. He was out at the time herding his cattle, so the children set to work to sweep out his hut, and then drank his milk.

In the evening when the cattle returned to the kraal, the children hid themselves in the devil's bed, i.e. they covered themselves with the grass which had been thrown in the corner of the hut. When the devil arrived, and saw that the place had been swept clean, and his milk drunk, he wept, and said, "Ah! Have the spirits of my mother's hut visited me? I will hang myself tomorrow morning."

The children remained silent in the bed while the devil was talking; but when he went to milk his cows, the boy got up and said: "I must go and get some milk." His sister tried to dissuade him, and reminded him that if the devil saw him he would eat them both. He went, nevertheless, and when the devil left his cows for a few minutes, the boy seized a gourd, and brought it into the hut, where he emptied it with his sister, after which he put it back in the place where he had found it. On the devil's return, he said: "Ah! Have the spirits of my mother's hut come to drink my milk? I will hang myself tomorrow morning."

---

[1] "The tail of small beads."

Having put the calves in their shed, the devil entered the hut, and lit a fire at the entrance. His tail was so long that he was unable to put it in the hut, so he left it outside, and fanned the fire with it, and blew the sparks into a flame with his back. When the boy saw what the devil was doing, he laughed, and the devil said: "Ah! the spirits of my mother's hut are laughing at me."

The next morning, the devil fastened a cord round his neck, and hanged himself. When he was dead, the boy cut off the long tail, and took it away with him. The children then started off to retrace their steps of the day before, driving the devil's cattle before them.

They had not gone far before they met a number of hyenas who asked the boy whose caravan he was traveling with. On hearing that it was Sae-Kidongoi's, they were much alarmed, and asked whether the devil would overtake them if they were to run away. The boy told them that if they were to run for four days they would escape, but to show that the devil was not far off, he pointed to some dust which was rising up behind the cattle, and told them that that was Sae-Kidongoi's tail. The hyenas at once fled, and the children pursued their way without further molestation.

When they stopped for the night, they were visited by some lions, who asked them whom the cattle belonged to. The boy answered: "They belong to nobody, you had better eat them; but if you do, you will never boast again."

The lions were surprised at this reply, and said: "Why should we never boast again? Is there anything that we fear except Sae-Kidongoi?"

The boy then asked them: "Don't you believe these cattle are Sae-Kidongoi's?"

The lions were incredulous, and told him to show them the devil. The boy replied: "He is asleep." But he went to where a calf was lying, and tied one end of the devil's tail to it. The tail was so long that when one stood at the other end it was impossible to see that it had been fastened to the calf. The boy then returned to the lions and called them. One of them went with him, but when he saw Sae-Kidongoi's tail he fled and the others followed him.

The next morning the boy followed the cattle trail until he reached his father's kraal. He made his own kraal, and then went and killed his father and stepmother, after which he combined and kept the two herds.

Both he and his sister became adults, when certain ceremonies were performed. They then married and lived happily ever afterwards.

The Warriors and the Monkeys

Some warriors once wished to go and raid, so they consulted a medicine man before starting, and were told that if they killed any monkeys on the road, the expedition would prove a failure.

One of the warriors was a coward, and when he heard what had been predicted, he made up his mind if a chance presented itself to kill a monkey.

On the road the warriors saw two monkeys and called one another's attention to them. The coward also saw them, and stayed behind on the pretext of having broken his sandal. He waited until his companions had passed on, and then killed one of the monkeys which being ill was unable to run away. He afterwards rejoined the other warriors, and they continued their journey.

In the meantime the monkey which had escaped returned to its dead comrade and lamented its loss. "O! my brother," it said, "I tried to persuade you to run away, and you said you were not able. Then the cursed one came and killed you. O! my brother."

When the warriors reached the country they intended to attack, they saw one of the inhabitants sitting under a stone trapping rock-rabbits. They crept up to him and threw a club at him. Although the club hit its mark, the man only complained of the flies that bit him. Another club was thrown with a like result. The man then turned round, and seeing the warriors, sprang at them, and although unarmed put them to flight.

The warriors at once knew that the coward had killed the monkey contrary to the medicine man's advice, and they put him to death on the spot.

Konyek and His Father[2]

A big dance was once held at which many warriors and maidens were present. Towards evening the dancers despersed, and each warrior selected one or more of the girls to accompany him home.

One of the men, a particularly handsome and well-built fellow, went away with three sisters. On leaving, he asked the girls where they would like to go, and they told him they wished to accompany him to his kraal. He said that it was a long way off, but they replied that that did not matter.

They started off, and after walking some distance they approached the kraal. The girls noticed some white things scattered about on the ground, and asked the warrior what they were. He said that they were his sheep and goats; but when they reached their destination, they saw that they were human bones. They entered the warrior's hut, and the girls were surprised to find that he lived quite alone.

It transpired later that this warrior was in reality a devil who ate people; but it was not known, as he concealed his tail under his garment. He had even eaten his mother, and had thrown her bones into the heap of grass which formed the bed.

Shortly after their arrival at the hut, the warrior went outside, leaving the girls alone. A voice, which came from the bed, startled them by asking them who had brought them there. They replied that the warrior had brought them, whereupon the voice told them to open the mattress. The girls threw off the top layer of grass exposing the bones to view. The voice, which came from the bones, then related that she had been the warrior's mother,

---

[2] The origin of this tale is doubtful. It is well known throughout Masailand, and is probably of ancient date; but as the nudity on the part of the men is notorious, it would be impossible for a Masai warrior to hide his tail, if he had one, under his cloth or skin.

Among the Nilotic tribes it is a common practice for women to wear a tail of strings behind, and among the peoples visited by Schweinfurth, and described in *The Heart of Africa,* we find that the Dyoor men wore tails of calf skin, and the Bongo "tails, like black horses' tails, composed of the bast of the Sanseviera." The Bongo men and their neighbors, the Mittoo, the Nyam-Nyam, and the Kredy, "also wear an apron of some sort of skin." These people are, or were, cannibals.

and that he had become a demon, and eaten her. The girls asked
the bones what they should do, and the voice spoke as follows:
"The warrior will come presently and bring you a sheep. Accept
it. He will then go outside again, and, having shut the door, sit
down there. Make a hole in the wall and pass out. If you are
asked what the knocking is, say that you are killing the sheep."

Everything took place as the voice had predicted, and the girls
made a hole in the wall of the hut through which they passed and
escaped. When they reached the road, however, one of them suddenly remembered that she had left her beads behind. Her sisters
told her to go and fetch them while they waited for her. She
returned to the hut, but met the warrior, who asked her if he
should eat her or make her his wife. She thanked him for giving
her the choice, and said she preferred the latter.

They lived together for a considerable period, and after a time
the woman presented the demon with a son whom they named
Konyek. From the day of his birth Konyek accompanied his father
on his journeys to the forest in quest of people to devour; and
while the man and the boy ate human beings, they took home with
them for the woman goats and sheep to eat and cows to milk.

One day one of the woman's sisters came to the kraal to visit
her. As Konyek and his father were both absent when she
arrived, the two women sat and talked until it was time for the
visitor to depart. The weather looked threatening as she rose to
take her leave, and Konyek's mother cried out to her not to go
to the tree in the middle of the plain, should it rain, for it was
her husband's and son's custom to rest there on their way home.
But the woman hurried away without paying attention to her sister's warning, and when it came on to rain a little later, she ran
to the tree in question, which was a baobab, and climbed up into
it. She had not been there long before Konyek and his father
arrived upon the scene, and stood underneath the tree to get
shelter from the rain. Their appearance recalled to the woman
her sister's words, and she was greatly alarmed.

Konyek gazed up into the tree, and remarked that there was
something peculiar about it, but his father said it was only
because it was raining hard. Shortly afterwards, however,
Konyek saw the woman, and called out: "There is my meat."

The woman was forced to descend, and she gave birth to twins. Konyek picked up the children, and said: "I will take these kidneys to mother to roast for me."

When it stopped raining the two returned home, and Konyek asked his mother to roast his kidneys for him. But the woman knew at once that her sister had been put to death, and she hid the children in a hole in the earth, roasting instead two rats. When they were ready, Konyek went to the fire, picked them up off the stones, and ate them, grumbling at the same time because they were so small. His mother pretended to be very annoyed at this, and turning to her husband, complained of what their son had said. The old man told her not to mind the boy as he was a liar.

The woman fed and tended the children, who were both boys, and gradually they grew. One day she asked her husband to bring her an ox, which, she said, she wished to slaughter and eat. Konyek on hearing this request at once pricked up his ears, and remarked: "It really amuses me to hear of a woman who wants to eat an ox all by herself. I think those kidneys of mine have something to do with this matter." However, the two men searched for an ox which they procured and brought back with them. They slaughtered the animal, and left the meat with the woman, after which they went for a walk in the forest.

As soon as they had departed, the woman let the children come out of their hole and gave them the ox to eat. They ate till sunset, when she sent them back again to their hiding place.

Konyek and his father returned shortly afterwards, and the former being very sharp at once noticed the small footmarks on the ground. "I wonder," he said, "what those small and numerous footmarks are. They are certainly not mine." His mother, however, stoutly insisted on the marks having been made by herself or by the two men, and in this she received her husband's support. Being annoyed with Konyek on account of the way he treated his mother, the old man killed him and ate him. But he immediately came to life again, and cried out: "There, I have come back again."

As time passed on the children grew up, and their aunt asked them one day if they knew that the people who lived in the same kraal with them were in reality demons and cannibals. She also inquired if, in the event of her being able to obtain weapons from her husband, they could put Konyek and his father to death. The boys replied that they could, but asked the woman what she would say if her husband wanted to know why she required the weapons. She told them that she would say she wanted them to protect herself against any enemies who might come.

When Konyek and his father next returned home, the woman asked her husband if he would procure two spears, two shields, and two swords for her, "for," she said, "I am always here alone, and if any enemies come, I wish to be able to fight with them." Konyek remarked that he had never before heard of a woman who wanted men's weapons, and said he thought that those kidneys which he had brought his mother to roast for him must have something to do with this request. Notwithstanding Konyek's protest the old man obtained for his wife the weapons she required. When he had given them to her, she fetched an ox hide, and asked the two men to lie down on the ground while she stretched the hide over them and pegged it down. She told them that when she was ready she would cry out and see if the enemy came, in which case they could assist her. She pegged the ox hide down securely, and asked them if they could get out. Konyek found a hole and began to crawl out, but his mother told him to get in again, and she pegged it down once more. She then raised her voice, and called to the children, who came from their hiding place, and killed Konyek and his father.

As Konyek was dying, he said to his parent: "Did I not tell you so, and you said I lied?"

The boys, after killing the two devils, took their aunt away to their father's kraal.

The Old Man and His Knee

There was once an old man who was unmarried and lived alone in his hut.

One night he went to sleep, and when he awoke in the morning, he found his knee was greatly swollen. There was nobody to attend to him, so he kept quiet as he thought he only had a boil. After remaining thus for six months, he asked himself how it was the boil did not come to a head so as to enable him to lance it. He waited two months more, and as it had not come to a head, he said to himself: "Even if it kills me, I will lance it." He therefore took his knife, and lanced it; and out came two children.

He looked after the children and fed them, and when they were old enough, he told them to sit by the door of the cave, while he went to look for food, and not to open to people they did not know.

On his return he sang:

"It is now soft, but not yet burst,
     My children of the knee.
Go, my little one, let me in,
     Open the door to me."

The children opened the door to him, and he entered, and gave them their food.

One day some of the old man's enemies came to the cave, and said to the children: "Open the door, children." But as the children refused, they decided to wait until the sun should set to see if the owner arrived.

The old man returned in the evening, and sang the usual song, whereupon the door was opened.

The enemies then elected to sleep where they were, and to go the next evening to sing the same song, and to kidnap the children. So the next evening they went to the cave and sang:

"It is now soft, but not yet burst,
     My children of the knee.
Go, my little one, let me in,
     Open the door to me."

As the voice, however, did not resemble their father's, the children refused to open the door.

The men then returned to their own country and consulted a medicine man. They told him they wanted to make their voices resemble an old man's in order that they could kidnap some children they had seen in the forest.

The medicine man told them to go back to where the children were, and to eat nothing on the road.

But before they reached the cave, they had eaten a lizard and an ant[3] which they found, thinking that these small things would not matter. On their arrival they sang the song, but the children did not recognize their father's voice, and refused to open the door. The enemies then returned to the medicine man's kraal, and, on being asked what they had eaten on the road, replied: "A lizard and an ant."

They were told to go again to the cave, and to pick up nothing whatever on the way, not even a small ant.

They did as they were told, and when they reached the cave they sang the song. The children, thinking it was their father, opened the door, whereupon the men entered and carried them off to their kraal.

In the evening the old man returned to the cave, and sang, but as he received no answer, he looked for the children. When he did not find them, he wept, and started off to search in the neighboring kraals.

He arrived at one kraal and sang, but received no reply. He then went on to the next one, and sang again, and the children recognized his voice, and wept. When their father heard them, he went outside, and shouted loudly. The people told him to stop, and said a spell had been put on the town, and that no stranger might enter without eating a certain medicine. They then put a stone in the fire, and when it was hot, told the old man to open his mouth and swallow the medicine. The old man opened his mouth, and the stone was thrown in, and killed him. After this the children of the knee remained in the kraal.

The Greed of the Old Man and His Wife

There was once upon a time an old man who lived in a kraal with his neighbors. And this old man had a wife and a small child, and he possessed a very fine ox.

---

[3] No Masai ever touches ants or lizards. All the Nilotic tribes, however, are very fond of white ants, while the Bongo and Nyam-Nyam, visited by Schweinfurth, "reckon as game everything that creeps and crawls," and eat caterpillars, worms, snakes, and crocodiles *(The Heart of Africa).*

One day he said to himself: "How shall I slaughter my ox?" and he said aloud to his wife: "My child! I will call the men and tell them that I am going to move. We can then slaughter our ox all by ourselves."

His wife agreed, and in the evening the old man blew his horn as a signal to his friends that he had something to tell them. His neighbors collected together, and he told them that he wished to move as the air did not agree with him. The others consented, and in the morning he saddled his donkeys, separated his cattle from the rest, and started off, accompanied by his wife, who was carrying the child.

When they had gone some distance, they halted and erected their kraal, after which they rested.

At dawn the next day the old man called his wife, and asked her why they had not yet slaughtered their ox. The woman replied: "My husband! How shall we manage to slaughter the ox? There are two things to be considered, the first is that we have no herdsman, and the second, that I am carrying the baby." The old man then said: "Oh, I know what we will do. I will stab the ox in the neck, then I will leave you to skin it, and I will carry the child to the grazing ground. But when you have skinned the animal, roast some meat so that it will be ready on my return."

The old man then killed the ox, after which he picked up his bow and quiver, put the child on his back, and drove the cattle to the grazing ground, where he herded them.

In the afternoon, as the child was asleep, the old man put it down in the grass, and went to drive back the cattle, for they had wandered far. But when he returned to the spot where he had left the child, he was unable to find it, so he decided to set light to the grass, "for," he thought, "when the fire reaches the child, it will cry, and I will run to the place and pick it up before it is burnt." He made a fire with his fire sticks, and the fire traveled to where the child was. He ran to the spot, but when he reached it, he found that the child was dead.

The old man had left his wife in the morning skinning the ox. And while she was skinning it—she had just reached the dewlap—the knife slipped, and she stabbed herself in the eye. She went and lay down, and the birds came and finished the meat.

After the child was burnt, the old man drove the cattle to the kraal, and when they were opposite to the gate, he heard his wife weeping, and saying: "Oh, my eye!" He therefore asked her who had told her the news.

"What news?" she inquired.

"The child has been burnt," he replied.

The woman exclaimed: "Oh, my child!"

The old man then asked where his meat was, and his wife informed him that the birds had eaten it, whereupon he cried out: "Oh, my meat!"

They both wept, the old man crying: "Oh, my meat!" and the woman: "Oh, my child! Oh, my eye!"

Look well at these people. It was for their greed that they were punished; they lost their child and their ox, the woman lost her eye, and they had to return in shame to their former home.

The Woman and the Children of the Sycamore Tree

There was once a woman who had no husband, and she lived for many days in trouble. One day she said to herself: "Why do I always feel so troubled? It is because I have neither children nor husband. I will go to the medicine man and get some children."

She went to the medicine man and told him she was unhappy owing to the fact that although she had now grown old she had neither husband nor children. The medicine man asked her which she wanted, husband or children; and she told him she wanted children.

She was instructed to take some cooking pots—three or as many as she could carry—and to search for a fruit-bearing sycamore, to fill the pots with the fruit, to put them in her hut, and to go for a walk.

The woman followed out these instructions implicitly. She gathered the fruit, filled the pots, placed them in her hut, and went for a walk till the evening.

On arriving near the kraal, she heard the sound of voices and asked herself: "Why does one hear the voices of children in the kraal?" She approached nearer, and found her hut filled with children, all her work finished, the boys herding the cattle, the hut swept clean by the girls, the warriors singing and dancing on the common, and the little children waiting to greet her. She thus became a rich woman, and lived happily with her children for many days.

One day, however, she scolded the children, and reproached them with being children of the tree. They remained silent and did not speak to her; then, when she went to see her friends in the other kraals, they returned to the sycamore tree, and became fruit again. On her return to her own kraal, the woman wept bitterly when she found it empty, and paid another visit to the medicine man, whom she taxed with having spirited away her children.

The medicine man told her that he did not know what she should do now, and when she proposed to go and look at the sycamore tree, he recommended her to try.

She took her cooking pots to the tree and climbed up into it. But when she reached the fruit they all put forth eyes and stared at her. This so startled her that she was unable to descend, and her friends had to come and help her down.

She did not go to the tree again to search for children.

The Father of Marogo

There was once upon a time an old man called "The Father of Marogo" who was a great glutton. He had only one daughter, Marogo, but he disliked the child very much as he had to provide food for her.

After a while his wife gave birth to a second child, and about the same time Marogo was married, and moved to her husband's kraal. The old man then lived alone with his wife and baby.

One day Marogo sent a messenger to invite her parents to come on the morrow to her husband's kraal as they intended to slaughter a bullock. When the messenger arrived, Marogo's father was away from home attending to his cattle, so the message was delivered to his wife, who replied that they accepted.

The cattle returned in the evening, and the woman said to her husband: "Father of Marogo, Marogo has sent us a message."

He replied, "What did the hag say?"

The woman rebuked him for calling their daughter names, and told him that their son-in-law was going to slaughter a bullock the next day, and that Marogo had bidden them to the feast.

Marogo's father was delighted, and cried out: "Ah! my dear Marogo. Anybody could see that she is my daughter."

The next morning they started for their son-in-law's kraal, and on the road came to a big river. The woman, who had been carrying the baby, called out to her husband to help her. The old man told her to bring him the child and he would take it across; at the same time he gave his wife his clay pot, which he had exchanged for a goat, and instructed her not to let the water sweep it away.

He then entered the river, but before he reached the middle, he let go the child and the current carried it away. The woman burst into tears, but her husband told her to be quiet as the child would be picked up lower down the stream. He called out to some imaginary people, and when the sound ceased echoing among the trees, he said: "Seize this child." The echo came back to them, and he asked his wife if she heard the reply, after which he proposed that they should go on.

As they were leaving the bank, the woman asked him where the men were who had picked up the child. Marogo's father replied: "You women are such fools! Even if this child is lost, won't you bear another?"

They continued their journey, and when they arrived near Marogo's kraal, the old man saw the people slaughtering the bullock. As his wife was some way behind, he beckoned to her with his club in order to point out to her that the feast had commenced. He thought he was only beckoning to her, but as his wife came up to him, he hit her on the head with the club, and made the blood gush forth.

He was sorry for what he had done, and picked up some earth which he plastered on the wound. He told his wife not to let the people they were visiting know that he had hit her; "and," he added, "if you are offered plenty of meat, don't refuse. Put it on one side, and give it to me afterwards, for I shall not get enough to eat. Now that you have no child, you can take home whatever you don't eat."

They stayed in their daughter's kraal until it was time to return, and the woman took away some of the meat that was left over for her husband to eat at home.

The Two Wives and the Twins

There was once upon a time a man who had two wives. By one wife he had no family, but by the other he had several children.

The latter on one occasion gave birth to twins, and great was her joy when she heard that both the children were boys. The barren woman, however, was so jealous that she made up her mind to do something that would turn her husband's love for the happy mother to hatred. She took the babies while their mother was sleeping, and cut their fingers, after which she rubbed some of the blood on their mother's mouth. She then put the children into a drum, which she threw into the river, and called to the other inhabitants of the kraal to come and look at the woman who had eaten her offspring. The men came, and, seeing the blood, believed the story, especially as the children were nowhere to be found. The old man was at first uncertain what to do with the supposed murderess; but after a while he called her to him and told her that as a punishment she should herd donkeys for the rest of her days.

The drum in which the woman had put the children was carried along by the current to another country, and some old men who were sitting on the bank of the river outside their kraal saw it as it was floating down the stream. The one who saw it first claimed it as his, while one of the others claimed the contents, whatever they might be. The drum was fished out of the water, and when it was opened the two babies were brought to light. The old man who had claimed the contents of the drum took the children to his hut, and fed them, and brought them up as his own sons.

In course of time the boys grew up, were circumcised, and became warriors. They had received the nickname "Sons of the drum" from their playmates and fellow warriors, and as they did not understand the meaning, they asked the older people why it had been given them. On hearing the story of their being found in a drum in the river, they decided to pay a visit to the country of their birth; and so as not to arrive empty-handed, they thought it would be well to first of all undertake a raid, and capture some cattle. They shortly afterwards started off on a raiding expedition, and succeeded in lifting a herd of cattle. They then passed through a forest, arriving eventually in another country where signs of habitation soon became evident. They had not proceeded far before they came upon a woman herding donkeys outside a kraal. That a woman should undertake so menial a task surprised them to such an extent that they went up to her and accosted her. "How is it," they asked, "that you are herding the donkeys? Is this not the children's work?"

The woman replied: "It is painful to me to explain to you, my children, why I do this work." She, however, proceeded to tell them the pathetic story of her life. She related how her husband had had two wives, and while the other one was barren, she herself gave birth to several children. She spoke of her twins, and described how the other woman had come to her while she was asleep, cut her babies' fingers, and smeared the blood on her mouth. She went on to say that the children were put into a drum by the other wife, and thrown into the river; and she dwelt on the punishment to which she had been sentenced.

The warriors on hearing this account said to the woman: "We are your children, look at our fingers," and they related to her the story which had been told them of their being found in the drum.

The woman at once recognized her sons, and, at their request, left the donkeys and milked their cows. The donkeys went back to the kraal by themselves in the evening, and the people asked one another where "the donkey woman" was, this being the name which had been given to the herdswoman.

On the morrow she was seen dressed in new clothes, and the

inhabitants of the kraal asked if "the donkey woman" had found the sons she had eaten. When her husband saw her, he wished to beat her; but he was deterred by the two warriors, who requested him to call a meeting of the men of the kraals so that they might talk with them.

The men came, and it was found that the warriors were the old man's sons.

The old man then wished to kill his barren wife, but his sons told him to give her the same work to do which he had formerly given to their mother. This he did, and the guilty woman was sentenced to herd donkeys for the rest of her life.

The Caterpillar and the Wild Animals

Once upon a time a caterpillar entered a hare's house when the owner was absent. On his return the hare noticed the marks on the ground, and cried out: "Who is in my house?" The caterpillar replied in a loud voice: "I am the warrior son of the long one, whose anklets have become unfastened in the fight in the Kurtiale country. I crush the rhinoceros to the earth, and make cow's dung of the elephant! I am invincible!"

The hare went away saying: "What can a small animal like myself do with a person who tramples an elephant underfoot like cow's dung?" On the road he met the jackal, and asked him to return with him and talk with the big man who had taken possession of his house. The jackal agreed, and when they reached the place, he barked loudly, and said: "Who is in the house of my friend the hare?"

The caterpillar replied: "I am the warrior son of the long one, whose anklets have become unfastened in the fight in the Kurtiale country. I crush the rhinoceros to the earth, and make cow's dung of the elephant! I am invincible!" On hearing this the jackal said: "I can do nothing against such a man," and left.

The hare then fetched the leopard, whom he begged to go

and talk with the person in his house. The leopard, on reaching the spot, grunted out: "Who is in the house of my friend the hare?" The caterpillar replied in the same manner as he had done to the jackal, and the leopard said: "If he crushes the elephant and the rhinoceros, he will do the same to me."

They went away again, and the hare sought out the rhinoceros. The latter, on arriving at the hare's house, asked who was inside, but when he heard the caterpillar's reply, he said: "What, he can crush me to the earth! I had better go away then."

The hare next tried the elephant, and asked him to come to his assistance, but on hearing what the caterpillar had to say, the elephant remarked that he had no wish to be trampled underfoot like cow's dung, and departed.

A frog was passing at the time, and the hare asked him if he could make the man who had conquered all the animals leave his house. The frog went to the door and asked who was inside. He received the same reply as had been given to the others, but instead of leaving, he went nearer, and said: "I, who am strong and a leaper, have come. My buttocks are like the post, and God has made me vile."

When the caterpillar heard this, he trembled, and as he saw the frog coming nearer, he said: "I am only the caterpillar."

The animals who had collected near seized him, and dragged him out; and they all laughed at the trouble he had given.

The Warrior and the Lumbwa[4]

Once while the Masai warriors were slaughtering a bullock in the woods, their enemies, the Lumbwa, suddenly appeared at the kraal, and drove off the cattle that were grazing near at hand, killing at the same time the boy who was herding them.

A young girl, the sister of the owner of the cattle, on hearing

---

[4] The Lumbwa Masai or 'l-Oikop, resident in German East Africa [Tanganyika].

the news, ran to the slaughterhouse to call her brother. On her arrival she cried to the warriors: "O ye who are feasting! The dust rises in the direction of Lumbwa; the black and white cow is on the point of giving birth; the small calves have blotches on the sides of their heads; the bulls' humps move to and fro; and the child's body lies by the wayside. Ye who are wearing your goatskin aprons, and are ready for the fray, come!"

The warriors told her that her brother was not there, and advised her to go some distance further to a spot where others were also slaughtering. She started off again, and after a time found her brother, who treated the matter very lightly. On hearing what had occurred he called to his servant, Rindi, and told him to bring his sandals and spear.

Now this warrior was such a giant that his servant was unable to lift his weapons or sandals, and was obliged to roll them over and over until he reached the spot where his master was waiting. Some days elapsed after the theft of the cattle before the warrior was ready to start off in pursuit of the enemy, and then he was only accompanied by his servant.

After proceeding a short distance they arrived at a spot where the cow had cast its calf, and some way further on they reached a pond, near which some milk had been spilt. The warrior told his servant to taste this milk in order that he might know how far ahead of them the enemy was. Rindi tried the milk, and said it had been there two days. They continued their journey, and later on came to a lake where they found some more milk. Rindi tasted this too, and said it had been there since the preceding day.

The next morning they again saw some milk by the road, and this Rindi declared to have been spilt the night before.

On they went again, and during the course of the day came upon some more milk, which they found to be quite fresh. Rindi on tasting it asked the warrior if he could not see the Lumbwa as they could only be a short distance in front of them.

Shortly after this they came up with the enemy, and after a fight the warrior killed them all, and recovered his cattle, which he drove back to his kraal.

The Boy and His Brother
and Their Song

There once lived an old man who had two wives, and by each
wife he had a son. One of the wives died, and the old man told
the other one to look after both children.

The boys loved one another very much, and always went
together to herd their father's cattle. They had their own pet
cow, which they called the Dapple-gray, and when they wanted
to milk her they only had to sing the following song:

> "Child of my father, brother dear,
>> She yields her milk, our Dapple-gray,
> She yields it though no calf is near,
>> This song of mine she can't gainsay.

> "Into my mouth I milk thee not,[5]
>> Dear Dapple-gray, there's nought to fear,
> No gourd or calabash I've got,
>> I only, whom thou lov'st, am here."

After a time the woman took a great dislike to her stepson,
and made up her mind to get rid of him so that her own son
might have all the milk. She therefore dug a hole in the floor of
the hut, and said to the boy: "You whom God gave me, come
from the grazing ground at midday, and have your head shaved."

When the child arrived, his stepmother told him to go into
the hut, and bring the bag containing her razor from under the
bed. He entered the hut, and not seeing the hole which had
been dug in the floor, fell into it. The woman immediately covered in the hole by dropping a big stone into it.

In the evening the other boy returned with the cattle to the
kraal, and asked his mother where his brother was. The woman
replied that she had shaved him a short while before, and that

---

[5] It is a common practice among Masai herdsmen to milk their cows directly
into their mouths.

he had returned to the grazing ground. When she was told that he had not been seen, she wept and cried out: "My child is lost."

As nothing was heard of the boy that evening, it was assumed that he was dead. His brother was much distressed, and during the greater part of the next day while herding the cattle he wept and sang their everyday song.

In the evening he drove the cattle back to the kraal, singing as he went, and when he was outside his mother's hut, he heard his brother singing as well. He listened, and went to the door of the hut, where he sang again. His brother replied, and he heard the voice distinctly. He entered the hut, took away the stone, and rescued the boy.

The mother was looking after the calves at the time, and letting them go to the cows one at a time to be fed. On her return to the hut she was greatly surprised to see her stepson, and asked where the child came from. Her son answered: "He has come from the forest."

The next morning the boy sharpened a sword, and when his mother left her hut, he cut her throat. His half-brother, who had been put in the pit for nothing, was thus avenged, while the woman paid for her sin with her life.

The Ostrich Chicks[6]

There was once upon a time an ostrich, which, having laid some eggs, hatched them, and reared the chicks.

One day a lion came, and took the chicks away, and hid them. The mother bird followed the thief, and demanded her young ones; but the lion refused to give them up, and drove her away. She appealed to the counselors, but they were afraid of the lion, and decided that the chicks were his. The ostrich then went to call

---

[6] There are several Masai stories somewhat similar to this one. In all of them the lion is outwitted by the mongoose, who escapes by a second exit from an anthill.

a meeting of all the animals. When she arrived at the place where the mongoose lived, he told her to go and dig a hole under an anthill with two exits. This she did, and then collected all the animals at this spot. Like the counselors, however, they feared the lion, and said the chicks were his. When it came to the mongoose's turn to be asked, he cried out: "We have never seen hairs beget feathers. Think what you are saying. The chicks are the ostrich's." And having said that, he jumped down the hole under the anthill, and escaped at the other end. The lion jumped after him, and not knowing of the second exit, waited for him to come out of the hole by which he had entered. As time wore on, the lion became hungry, but he still kept watch, for he thought that if he went to search for food the mongoose would get away. At length he died, and the ostrich recovered her chicks.

The Crow Who Married a Woman

There was once upon a time a crow who made love to a woman. When he had given the woman's father the customary present, viz. three heifers and two young bulls, and brewed some honey wine, he was allowed to marry her. He took his wife away with him, and went to live in a wood.

At the end of a year the woman asked the crow where his kraal was, but he refused to tell her, nor would he vouchsafe a reply when she asked him, as she did daily, when they were going to his home.

One day the crow told her to climb up a tree, and to wait for him there while he went to cut some firewood for her. She did as she was bid, and when she reached the top, she sang and wept.

Just at this time the woman's former lover, who with her brothers was returning from a raid, passed near the tree. The lover recognized the singing, and told his friends that he heard their sister's voice. They laughed at him, and said they supposed the loss of their sister had turned his head. However, when they listened, they admitted that it was their sister's voice that they heard, and they started off to search for her. They found her in the tree, and asked her who had put her there. She replied that she had been sold to the crow who was at that moment collecting firewood. They told her not to come down when the crow returned, and then went away and hid.

Shortly afterwards the crow came back with the firewood, and called out to his wife to descend. She refused, however, even though he threatened to fetch her down.

While the two were disputing, the woman's brothers and lover emerged from their hiding place, and fought with the crow, whom they succeeded in putting to death. They then escorted her back to their kraal.

The Hare and the Hyena and the Lioness's Cave

The hare once met the hyena, and proposed that they should go for a walk. They went for a walk together, and then separated, after which the hare went to the lioness's cave, and found it closed. She cried out: "Stone, open," and the stone rolled away from the mouth of the cave. She entered and said: "Stone, close," and the stone returned to its place. She then proceeded to the room where the lioness stored her fat, after which she went to the room where the meat was kept, and having had enough to eat, she returned to the entrance, told the stone to open, and when she had passed out, to close once more.

Feeling hungry again later she returned to the cave. On the road she met the hyena, who asked her where she came from, and why her mouth was oily. The hare denied that her mouth was oily, but as the hyena persisted in his statement, she told him to rub ashes on his mouth, and it would become as beautiful as hers. The hyena did as he was recommended, but no change took place in his appearance. The hare next suggested washing it with water, and afterwards with urine; but although the hyena tried both, his mouth remained as dry as before. The hyena then said: "Please tell me where you go and feed." At first the hare refused to comply with his request, and said: "You are so foolish whenever you go anywhere, and are sure to be caught." But as the hyena would take no refusal, she consented to allow him to accompany her, and told him about the lioness's cave. "There are," she said, "five rooms. In the first the ashes are kept; in the next, the bones; in the third, the tough meat; in the fourth, the tender meat; and in the last, the fat." The hyena cried: "Get out of the way, take me there," and off they started.

When they arrived at the cave, the hare told the hyena that when he wanted the cave to open he must say: "Stone, open," and when he wanted it to shut: "Stone, close." The hyena cried out: "Stone, open," and the stone rolled aside. When they were inside, the hare said: "Stone, close," and it closed again.

The hyena at once started on the ashes, while the hare went to the room where the fat was kept. When the latter had had enough to eat, she returned to the entrance, and said she was going away. The hyena remonstrated with her as he was not nearly satisfied. After telling him how to get out of the cave, the hare went up to the stone, and said: "Stone, open," and again, when she was outside: "Stone, close."

When the hyena was alone, he went to the place where the bones were kept, after which he proceeded to the next room, where the tough meat was stored, and ate until he was satisfied. He then returned to the entrance, and said to the stone: "Stone, close," instead of "Stone, open." He repeated the words "Stone, close," several times, and could not understand why nothing happened.

At this juncture the lioness, the owner of the cave, returned, and said: "Stone, open." When the hyena heard her, he cried: "Ah! woe is me! That is what I wanted to say. Poor fellow that I am! Stone, open! Stone, open!"

The lioness entered, and said: "Shall I eat you, or shall I make you my servant?"

The hyena asked to be made her servant, and was told to look after the lioness's cub. He was also given a bone, and instructed to break it when the lioness had crossed four rivers. The hyena counted the lioness's footsteps, and when he calculated that she had crossed the four rivers, broke the bone. A chip flew at the cub's head fracturing its skull. Fearing that the lioness would kill him on her return, he searched for some hornets, and stuffed one up each of the cub's nostrils so that it might be supposed that it had been stung to death.

The lioness returned to her cave a short while afterwards, and called to the hyena to bring her cub. The hyena prevaricated for some time, and invented several excuses for not doing as he was told; but the lioness was firm, and the hyena had to pick up the cub and bring it to its mother. The lioness at once saw that it was dead, and told the hyena to take it outside. While he was doing this, he ate one of the cub's legs.

A little later he was again ordered to bring the cub to its mother, and then to take it away once more. He devoured another leg while carrying it away, and when the lioness called out to him a third time to bring the cub to her, he said the birds had eaten two of its legs. He then ate up the cub.

The lioness intended to punish the hyena for his misdeeds, and after tying him to a tree, went to get some sticks with which to beat him. As he was standing there, bound to the tree, some other hyenas bent on a raiding expedition passed close by, and one of them seeing him, asked him why he had been tied up in this manner. He replied that he was being punished for having refused to drink some oil which had some flies in it. The other hyena suggested that they should exchange places, and after untying the knots, he allowed himself to be bound to the tree instead, while the first hyena followed in the wake of the raiding party.

After a time the lioness returned, and commenced to flog the hyena, who cried out: "Stop, I will drink it now."

"Drink what?" said the lioness, and she commenced to flog him again.

"Oh! oh!" the hyena cried, "I will drink the oil with the flies in it."

The lioness then saw that this was not the hyena that had killed her cub.

The next morning the hyenas on their way back from their raid passed the cave, and the one that had killed the cub saw on the ground some strips of bark, which the lioness had spread out in the sun to resemble meat. "I will go to my master's kraal," quoth he, "for I see there has been a kill." On reaching the spot, however, he was seized by the lioness, who bound him to the tree once more, and then beat him to death.

After this the lioness returned to her cave, and said: "Stone, open." When the stone had rolled aside, and she had entered, she said: "Stone, close," and it closed again.

The Demon Who Ate People, and the Child[7]

There was once upon a time a demon who was greatly dreaded by the inhabitants of the country in which he lived owing to his principal food being human beings.

On one occasion he devoured a large number of people and cattle—so many, in fact, that he thought he had exterminated the whole tribe. One woman, however, succeeded in hiding herself with her child in a pit, and after the demon had taken his departure she returned to the kraal and collected together all the food that had been left there.

The child was brought up in the pit, and when he was old enough to understand, his mother told him the story of the demon. For some time he did not venture away from the hiding place, but after a while he made a bow and some arrows, and went for a walk. He shot a small bird, which he took back with him to the pit, and asked his mother if that was the demon. On being told that it was not, he went out again and shot another bird, and after that a Thomson's gazelle. He continued his search for a long time, and shot all kinds of things in the hope of killing the demon, but when he showed them to his mother, he found that he had not been successful.

The woman repeatedly urged her son not to leave the pit as they were the sole survivors of the tribe, but the boy was deter-

---

[7] A Taveta Tale. The people of Taveta are nearly allied to the Masai, many of them being actually descended from that race. An account of their history and customs, by the author, was published in the *Journal of the African Society*, No. 1, October, 1901.

mined if possible to shoot the demon. One day he searched for a number of arrows and spears which he took to the top of a tree. He then climbed with his mother into the tree and lit a fire in the branches to attract the demon's attention. When the demon saw the smoke, he was greatly surprised, as he thought he had eaten all the inhabitants of the country. Having procured some axes, he went to the spot, and called out to the child and his mother to descend. As they refused to comply with his order, he commenced to cut down the tree. The boy shot him twice with his arrows, but the demon only thought he was being bitten by gadflies. As the arrows continued to hit him, however, he had to give up his intention of cutting down the tree, and shortly afterwards he lay down to die.

When he felt that his end was approaching, he said to the child: "When I am dead, cut off my little finger, and your cattle will be restored to you. Then, cut off my thumb, and you will get back your people. After that cut open my face, and one man will come out."

Having said this, he died, and the boy descended from the tree and cut off his fingers and thumb, from the stumps of which all the people and cattle that had been eaten emerged. The face was then cut open, and one man appeared.

The people returned with their cattle to their former kraals, and held a consultation at which it was decided to appoint the boy chief.

After some time had elapsed, the man who had been taken from the devil's face asked the chief to put him back again. The others argued with him, and told him that he was much better off now that he had been liberated, but their arguments availed nothing, and the chief, seeing that the man would take no refusal, asked to be given a month in which to consider the matter.

Knowing that the discontented man was very fond of tobacco, the chief planted some, and when it ripened, he went to watch it. As he expected, the man saw the tobacco, and picked a leaf. The chief called out to him to return it to the plant, but as the thief was unable to do this, he was taken to the kraal, where a meeting was held. Matters having been explained to those present, the thief was again called upon to replace the leaf. When he admitted his inability to do as he was required, the chief remarked that he too was unable to put him back in the demon's face.

Everybody appreciated the wisdom of the argument, and they all lived happily together ever afterwards, respecting their chief and loving one another.

The Two Dorobo

Two Dorobo brothers once went out hunting together, and came upon a large herd of buffaloes. The elder one told his brother to conceal himself while he went to drive the animals. The drive was successful, and the buffaloes passed so close to the younger Dorobo that he was able to shoot three of them.

The elder brother then told the other one to go and drive the herd while he hid himself. The buffaloes came past the spot again, but although the hunter shot at them, he failed to hit them. The animals were by this time so scared that they fled.

The three buffaloes which had been killed were quickly skinned, and the meat carried off to the kraal. When this task was finished, the hunters started off again.

On arriving at a forest, the elder brother said he would go on ahead as he knew the way. They proceeded in this manner until near their destination, when the elder one held aside a tree which bent down onto the road, telling his brother at the same time to pass. The latter feared that the tree might slip and hit him in the eye; but as his brother assured him that he would not let it go, he passed. His fears were, however, not groundless, for his brother let the tree swing back as he approached; it caught him in the face, and put out his eye. He said nothing, but he thought to himself: "I know the reason why my brother has put out my eye. It is on account of the buffaloes which I shot; and because of them he does not wish me to shoot again. But there is One who will avenge me."

They reached the place where the buffaloes were, and the elder Dorobo said to his brother: "Since you can no longer see, go and drive the buffaloes here for me to shoot."

The younger one did as he was told, and drove the herd to where his brother lay hid. The latter shot at them as they passed, but missed them. The younger one then expressed a wish to have the buffaloes driven for him in order to see if he could still shoot. At this proposal the elder one laughed, and said: "How can you with your one eye expect to hit them when I, who have both eyes, miss?" Nevertheless he went and drove the herd towards his one-eyed brother who succeeded in shooting four.

The elder Dorobo was so annoyed at this that he decided to kill his brother, and to carry off all the meat for his own children. He thought the best plan would be for his brother to sleep alone, when he could visit him during the night and shoot him. So after they had skinned the animals, he said: "Since there is such a great quantity of meat, we had better divide it up now, and then each build his own hut; otherwise we might quarrel over it tomorrow."

They divided the meat into equal shares; each hunter built his own hut; and they went to lie down. But the younger one was mistrustful of his brother, and suspected foul play. Instead therefore of going to sleep, he took one of the buffalo legs, wrapped his garment round it, and laid it on the grass which he had cut for a bed, while he went to lie down on the bare ground.

In the middle of the night the elder Dorobo came stealthily into the hut, and seeing the leg in the bed, thought it was his brother. He sat down, took careful aim, let fly his arrow, and shot the leg.

The younger hunter had been watching him all the time, and thought to himself: "If my brother shoots at the leg, I shall know that he really intends to kill me." As soon as he saw the arrow leave his brother's bow, and hit the leg, he shot his brother, and killed him.

He then picked up all the meat and took it home.

The Dorobo and the Giraffe

A Dorobo once went a-hunting, and saw a giraffe eating a small acacia tree. Other people had been unsuccessful in their attempts to kill this giraffe on former occasions, so the hunter thought it would be wise to have someone to help him. He therefore fetched a friend; but when he returned to the spot where he had left the giraffe, he found the animal had gone to the water to drink. The two men then thought out a plan of attack. It was agreed that the one who had first seen the animal should climb into a big acacia tree, and when it returned from the stream, jump on its back, and stab it in the neck. The other one was to hide himself near at hand in order to render any assistance that might be required.

The first Dorobo took his friend's knife, and climbed into the acacia. He remained there till midday, when the giraffe went to stand in the shade of the tree. As soon as it was near enough to him, the hunter jumped on its back, and clung to its neck, shouting at the same time to his friend, whom he called Le-pambito, to shoot the animal, and not to let it pass. The giraffe, much alarmed, dashed off at full speed, and Le-pambito was so amused at the sight of the animal with a man on its back that he roared with laughter. In fact he laughed so much that he fell down in a fit.

The giraffe continued its onward course, and the Dorobo in his excitement forgot that he had a knife in his belt until they had gone a considerable distance. When he remembered it, he unsheathed it, and stabbed the animal in the nape of the neck, thereby killing it.

He quickly skinned a portion of the beast, and took out the fat of the kidneys, with which he returned to look for his companion. He eventually found Le-pambito, and was surprised to see that he was dead, as he thought. He made a fire, roasted some of the fat, and put it near his friend's nostrils, in order to try and bring him back to life again. It had the desired effect, for Le-pambito came to himself, and cried out: "Do not finish it alone."

The two went to skin the dead giraffe, and when they had finished, they roasted a little of the meat, which they ate. The one who killed the giraffe then said to his friend: "I shall not let you have any of this meat for you did not help me to kill it." On hearing this, Le-pambito returned to the kraal.

When he arrived there, he met his companion's wife, who asked him if he had seen her husband. He replied: "No, but I hear that he has killed a giraffe. I also hear," he added, "that he is very angry with you, and when he returns, he is going to beat you."

The woman, thinking doubtless that it would be more prudent to go and stop with her friends until her husband's anger was appeased, left her hut. As soon as Le-pambito saw her depart, he entered the hut and waited for the other one to bring home his meat.

In the morning the Dorobo who had killed the giraffe arrived at the kraal with his first load of meat, which he passed into his hut through a hole in the wall at the back. To make sure that his wife was in the hut he called out to her, and Le-pambito replied, altering his voice to resemble a woman's. Satisfied that his meat was in safe hands, the Dorobo went back to the place where he had killed the giraffe, to fetch another load; and while he was absent his late companion carried off the meat to his own hut, after which he returned to wait for the rest. When several loads of meat had been thus brought to the hut, and afterwards taken by Le-pambito, and deposited in his own hut, the latter went to the woman whom he had frightened away by telling her that her husband was going to beat her, and told her that she might now go home as her husband was no longer angry with her.

She returned to her hut, and shortly afterwards her spouse came back to the kraal with the last load of meat. He called out to his wife to bring him a stool, that he might rest himself, and to fetch the snuff. After he had refreshed himself by taking some snuff, he told the woman to go and call his neighbors.

When they had arrived, the Dorobo inquired if the meat was ready. His wife was much perplexed at this request, and asked him what meat he alluded to. He replied: "Why, all the meat—the whole giraffe—which I have brought here." The woman, to his astonishment, said that she had not seen it.

Much exasperated he rose from his seat and flogged her, after which she told him between her tears what Le-pambito had done.

The Dorobo then realized that he had lost his whole giraffe owing to his selfishness.

PROVERBS AND SAYINGS

1. Why do you behave like a woman whose son has just married?
[A newly married man usually lives in his father's kraal for some months after his marriage, and a woman whose son has recently married may sit down and rest, as her daughter-in-law will do all the work.]

2. There is a Judge for him, and He will avenge me.
[A favorite saying when a person has been defeated in a fight.]

3. Flies have ears. *Also:* The night has ears.
["Walls have ears."]

4. The mouth which ate fat shall eat excrement, and that which ate excrement shall eat fat. Also: The slayer of the enemy has become a coward, and the poltroon has become a brave man.
["The last shall be first, and the first last."—Matt. xx. 16.]

5. There is not such a thing in the world as a sheep of many colors.
[A sheep of two or even three colors is common enough, but one of more than three colors is unknown. This saying is used to express incredulity at an improbable story.]

6. Coal laughs at ashes, not knowing that the same fate which has befallen them will befall it. *Also:* The firewood which has been cut ready for burning laughs at that which is being consumed.

7. He eats his food like a donkey.
[This is said of a man who has not had the two middle incisors of the lower jaw extracted, and whose mouth in consequence is supposed to resemble a donkey's.]

8. It is the same thing when a man is once there whether he has been called or whether he has come of his own free will.

9. They separate themselves like the huts of the zebra.
[Zebras of course have no huts. This saying is intended to imply, "They are scattered over the face of the earth."]

10. Everything has an end.

11. Events follow one another like days.

12. Actions [this Masai word also means "arrows"] come by the use of the legs.
[Double meaning: Long marches are inevitable before a raid can be successfully accomplished; and arrows are not fired without a person being there to fire them.]

13. He separates himself from his friends like a sick (*or* dead) donkey.
[A sick donkey stands apart from his fellow animals, and a dead donkey is thrown away. This saying is used when referring to a man who stands aloof from his companions.]

14. Being defeated and dying are the same.

15. A cow is as good as a man.
[If a man has a cow, and looks after it, he obtains riches, for the cow bears, and with the calves he is able to purchase a wife.]

16. Hide your mouthfuls of food.
[One should not disclose one's secret thoughts any more than one shows the food one is eating.]

17. He is like a hyena's sinew.
[A man who refuses to admit himself beaten is likened to a hyena's sinew, which is said to be tougher than that of any other animal.]

18. The cow said: "Do not lend me—give me away."
[It is notorious that animals which have been lent or pawned are not as well treated as those of the person they have been lent to. Hence the cow's request.]

19. The cow said: "Say as many words about me as I have hairs in my body."
[If you wish to sell me, strike a hard bargain, for a man who has paid a long price for me will treat me well.]

20. The hyena said: "It is not only that I have luck, but my leg is strong."
[I have luck, it is true, but I have had to work. "God helps those who help themselves."]

21. There is a dog in the gourd, and his ears prevent it from being closed.
[In the event of a man going to visit his friend's wife, he would first of

all ascertain whether the owner of the hut were at home. Should he see unmistakable signs of the husband's presence, he would move off consoling himself by quoting this proverb.]

22. Mountains do not meet.
[A favorite saying when people part company, and equivalent to, "We shall meet again." Cf. the Turkish proverb: "Mountain does not meet mountain, but man meets man."]

23. You have got what the son of En-gipika got in the deserted kraal, i.e. you are in a fix.
[The story told of the son of En-gipika is as follows. One day he was eating meat in the slaughterhouse when the place was suddenly attacked by the enemy. He managed to escape with his life and meat, but without his weapons, and he fled, hotly pursued by the enemy. He outstripped them, however, and after running some distance, entered a deserted kraal where he proposed to hide. But he soon discovered that he was not the only occupant, and a lion growled savagely at being disturbed. Thinking it more prudent under the circumstances to leave the deserted kraal, the son of En-gipika turned round to continue his flight, when he was horrified to see an enormous serpent coiled round the post of the gate, which was the only exit, darting out its head and tongue in his direction. In the distance too he could see the enemy rapidly approaching his hiding place. It is not related how the son of En-gipika escaped from the dilemma in which he found himself.]

24. You are as clever as Konyek.
[Konyek's biography was briefly sketched in the story entitled "Konyek and His Father." The Masai are fond of referring to him whenever anything of a cunning or clever nature has been performed. The constructor of the Uganda Railway, for instance, has been referred to as being on a par with him.]

25. You are proud like the dog of the warriors' kraal.
[The dogs that live in the warriors' kraals have a much happier existence than those that act as scavengers in the other kraals. Owing to the warriors' food consisting entirely of meat and milk, many bones and scraps are thrown to the dogs.]

26. Behold the people you are passing. The man is there, and the male, the woman and the female.
[All people are not alike, and if you watch you find that some of the passersby are good and others bad.]

27. You have given yourself airs like the illness which takes the warrior in the kraal of the married people.
[A warrior is supposed to be always in a perfect state of health, and if he is taken ill, he will hide himself in the woods or in a hut apart from the others. A disease which succeeds in overtaking him when on a visit to the married people,[1] and making him the laughingstock of all, may well be proud of itself!]

28. Cover the eye of the goat.
[When a goat is about to be strangled, it is thrown on its side, and the eye which is uppermost is covered with its ear, so that it shall not see what is happening. Similarly, if a raid is meditated on, secrecy must be observed beforehand.]

29. We begin by being foolish and we become wise by experience.

30. You are not like a child who when carried only presses on my back, you press on every part of my body.
[This saying is equivalent to, "I am weary of your company."]

31. He has not been shown to be dead.
[Do not believe in the report of a person's death until it is well founded. Unless an eyewitness tells you the news, receive it with caution.]

32. One finger will not kill a louse.
[The necessity for joint action. The Swahili have a similar proverb.]

33. A man does not know when he is well off; it is only when he is poor that he remembers the days of plenty.

34. A bull cannot bellow in two places at once.

35. A bargain cannot be held in the palm of the hand. *Also:* A lie cannot fill the palm.
[One hollow cannot fill another.]

36. When an event occurs, only a part of the truth is sent abroad; the rest is kept back.

37. It does not take as long to settle a quarrel as it takes a cow's udder to fill with milk after she has been covered.
[The combatants either fight until one is beaten, or the matter is settled amicably at once.]

---

[1] The warriors live in kraals apart from the married people.

38. Bravery is not everything, and however brave a man may be, two brave men are better.
["Dieu est toujours pour les gros bataillons."—Voltaire.]

39. The belly does not swell if a woman is not pregnant.
["There is no smoke without a fire."]

40. The nose does not precede the rest of the body.
[This expression is often used after a misfortune has befallen one, the idea being that if it were possible to send on one's nose ahead, one could have foreseen the danger that was being threatened and made preparations accordingly.]

41. The beast of prey cannot be hidden by the grass.
[A beast of prey (or a thief) can hide for a while, but in course of time it will be captured or killed. "Murder will out."]

42. He who comes from a strong clan won't lose his cattle.
[No matter how young or weak a child may be on his father's death, he is strong in his own kraal, for his friends will see that he inherits the cattle.]

43. The boaster will not cross the valley.
["Pride goes before a fall."]

44. Warriors and cripples remain apart.
["Birds of a feather flock together."]

45. Don't make a cloth for carrying a child in before the child is born.
["Don't count your chicks before they are hatched."]

46. Cheating and doing something by force are not the same.
[If a man has suffered wrong, he had better try and come to an arrangement with his aggressor instead of going to complain to the chiefs, for his enemy will not forget, and will avenge himself later.]

47. Life and death are not alike.

48. What does it matter whether a person is one's own child or somebody else's as long as he does his duty?
[The Swahili have similar proverb: "It is better to have a Kaffir who pleases you than a Mahommedan who displeases you."]

49. The buttocks and the ground do not remain long apart.
[One explanation of this proverb is that a man must sit down, and though he may walk about or lie down, he will sit on the ground again

later. Another theory is that it has in some way reference to the disposal of the dead. With the exception, however, of the medicine men and rich people, who are buried in shallow trenches, burial is unknown among the Masai. But it is perhaps a remarkable coincidence that the Tavetans,[2] who are closely allied to the Masai, and the Bari, Dinka, and Madi, who live nearly 1,000 miles away, and not very far from the country whence the ancestors of the Masai are believed to have hailed, bury their dead in a *sitting* posture.]

50. The zebra cannot do away with his stripes.
["Can the Ethiopian change his skin, or the leopard his spots?"—Jer. xiii. 23.]

51. Baboons do not go far from the place of their birth.
[Similarly with people: they may pay a visit to another country (and incidentally lift their neighbor's cattle), but they will afterwards return home.]

52. The bark of one tree will not adhere to another tree.
[People of one tribe cannot assimilate the customs of another.]

53. Having enough to eat and being in safety are two very different things, especially after a raid.

54. Persevering to accomplish an end and being able to do a thing are not the same: it is greater to persevere.
[But this proverb can also mean: Persevering to accomplish an end and being able to do a thing are not the same: many persevere. "Many are called, but few chosen."—Matt. xxii. 14.]

55. Nobody can say he is settled anywhere forever: it is only the mountains which do not move from their places.

56. Broken pieces of a gourd cannot be fastened onto a cooking pot.
[Similarly, people of different tastes disagree.]

57. You will not be beaten when you think before acting.
["Look before you leap."]

58. Do not repair another man's fence until you have seen to your own.

---

[2] See above, page 30, note 7.

59. Don't go to the plain without somebody to take the dust out of your eye.

[The necessity of joint action.]

60. Do not show the hawk your bow, or he will fly away.

61. Do not jump about, for there is no use in jumping about.

["More haste less speed."]

62. You are not like firewood which is burnt, you are always there.

[Said of a person whose presence has become a nuisance.]

63. Do not talk a great deal.

64. Don't tread on the post, i.e. don't be proud, like the father of many sons.

[A man with a large family may lie on his back all day long with his feet up against a post, and trouble about nothing. His wife and daughters see to the food and milk the cows, while his sons guard the cattle and sheep.]

65. Do not hasten thither, for you will tire yourself.

["More haste less speed."]

66. O God! give me shade that is not from a tree.

[Originally a prayer for a child, but now used for anything that is ardently desired. When the sun is hot, a mother protects her infant's head by covering it with the "kesen," or garment for tying the child onto her back. No woman wears this garment unless she has a baby, hence her prayer for shade.]

67. She is like Namelele (nickname given to a weak woman), but not because she has no milk: her child is so badly fed that it is knocked over by the weight of a bird.

[This is a term of reproach used to a woman if she does not look after and feed her children properly.]

68. He who separates the paths, etc.

[A common expression for the Almighty.]

69. She is treading against the post like one who is not allowed in the warrior's kraals.

[Unless a girl is well dressed, according to Masai ideas, and anoints her body from time to time with oil, she is not admitted into the warriors' kraals, and becomes a social outcast. She has nothing left her to do but lie on her back and put her feet up against a post. Unlike the old man who has many sons, however (*vide* proverb No. 64), this is considered an undignified position for a maiden.]

70. It is better to be poor and live long than rich and die young.

71. The old man cannot get milk from the cow that has recently borne, because his daughter has not looked after the calf whose legs are consequently weak.
[A saying applied by women to one of their number who is notoriously lazy.]

72. He is as proud as a child living at its grandmother's.
[Grandmothers are apt to spoil their grandchildren, and a naughty boy is not so likely to be whipped at his grandmother's as at home.]

73. Men may be partners, or may eat from the same dish, but they cannot tell what is passing through each other's minds.

74. Look, they are as numerous as the unripe fruit of the oseki tree.

75. If a stranger comes to stay with you, do not forget when you lay aside his weapons that he is hungry.
["It is ill talking between a full man and a fasting."]

Index to Proverbs and Sayings

RIDDLES

THE PROPOUNDER says, Oiyōte, Are you ready?
The others reply, E-eˉuo, He has come (i.e. It is, or we are, ready).

1. What do my warriors resemble when they stand on one leg?
Answer: The euphorbia tree.
[Masai men often stand on one foot and rest the other against the knee.[1] When in this position they are supposed to resemble the *Candelabra euphorbia,* which Sir H. Johnston has described as being "like a gigantic cabbage or cauliflower that has run to stalk, only to countless stalks, many-jointed, and of gouty thickness."]

2. What are my warriors like? I have many of them, and one goes out to look after the cattle.
Answer: The rafters of the hut.
[In Masai huts all the rafters are hidden except one which protrudes beyond the door. It is said to be watching the cattle.]

3. What are my warriors like when they stand in a circle, and one cannot see which is the first and which is the last?
Answer: The pegs which are being used for pegging out a skin.

4. I have three warriors. What is a discussion between two of them like if the third is not present?
Answer: The stones used for standing the cooking pots on at the fire.
[The cooking pots cannot be successfully balanced between two stones, and a discussion does not terminate if only two people take part in it.]

5. I have two skins, one to lie on and the other to cover myself with. What are they?

---

[1] This mode of resting, uncomfortable as it may appear, is widespread.

45

Answer: The bare ground and the sky.

6. I whistle, and they all come running from the forests. What am I?
Answer: The rain.

7. Why do you say you are ready to guess my riddle?
Answer: Because it is a discussion between you and me.

8. What does your mother resemble? She is long, and yet she does not reach up to a sheep's udder.
Answer: The road.

9. I went to bed and brought forth two sticks. What were they?
Answer: Twins.

10. We have moved our kraal and your mother has left behind her the palm of her hand which has been hung up in the hut. What is it?
Answer: The broom.
[The piece of hide which is used for sweeping away the dust and dirt is of so little value that when the inhabitants quit their kraal and move to a new grazing ground it is probably left suspended from the wall of the hut.]

11. We have moved our kraal, and your father has left behind him his garment. Where has he left it?
Answer: On the dunghill.
[A man would not leave his dressed skin behind him unless it were worthless, and it is obvious, therefore, that it has been thrown away.]

12. When your mother leaves her hut, what is to be seen issuing from her garments?
Answer: The leg of her child.
[Masai matrons carry their babies fastened onto their backs, and a small leg is often to be seen dangling down, while the child's body is hidden from view.]

13. Why does your mother use abusive language when she goes outside her hut?
Answer: Because she is a woman eating gum.
[Masai women are fond of chewing a gummy substance which exudes from certain trees. This makes their teeth stick together, and their jaws crack when they attempt to speak. If a person accosts them, and hears this noise, he may think the women are reviling him.]

14. What is a strip of hide like when the tip is wet?
Answer: A road which leads to the water.
[The poisoned heads of arrows are wrapped up in a strip of hide to keep the poison fresh. This strip is narrow and long, and it is wetted at one end with saliva to make it adhere.]

15. What escapes a prairie fire?
Answer: A bare spot on which no grass grows.

16. What meat rolls about as if in agony when it is being cooked?
Answer: Fat, for its eyes (bubbles) hurt it.

17. What is the thing which hides itself in its bed?
Answer: The louse which the boys uncover.

18. What hides itself against the wall of the hut?
Answer: The widow who was not present when blood was extracted from an ox.
[The Masai drink the hot frothing blood direct from the live cattle. After tying a leather ligature tightly round an animal's throat, an arrow is shot into one of the superficial veins of the neck. When the arrow is pulled out, the blood gushes forth, and is collected in gourds. The blood is drunk greedily by all present, but who will give any to the widow?]

19. What is the clammy thing which is always in your hut and which you don't notice?
Answer: The lizard.

20. That there; this here.
Answer: Drops of milk.
[*That there* is the drop of milk at the bottom of the gourd; this here is the drop when the gourd has been tipped up into the mouth.]

21. Why is the mother weak?
Answer: Because they did not catch the blood in the gourd.

22. What resembles a butterfly?
Answer: A garment with beads worked on it.
[It is only the best dressed girls who wear skins ornamented with beads, and when they move about from one hut to another, they are supposed to resemble butterflies.]

23. What will your hands be like if we meet after you have gone round that part of the mountain?
Answer: The lama fruit.

[This is a common wild fruit (*Ximenia americana,* L.) of which the
Masai are very fond. It stains everything a blood-red color.]

24. What is folding up the skins and going to Kinangop like?
Answer: The bitches' tails.

[This is a well-known saying among the Masai of Kilima Njaro.
Kinangop (or better, Kinokop or Kinobop) is the name of a subdistrict
near Naivasha, and is some 300 miles from Kilima Njaro. It is supposed that the way there would resemble a bitch's curly tail.]

MYTHS AND TRADITIONS

The Story of the Gods

THERE ARE TWO gods, a black one and a red one. The black god is good, and the red god malicious.

One day the black god said to the red one: "Let us give the people some water for they are dying of hunger."

The red god agreed, and told the other one to turn on the water. This he did, and it rained heavily.

After a time the red god told the black one to stop the water as sufficient rain had fallen.

The black god was, however, of opinion that the people had not had enough, so he refused.

Both remained silent after this, and the rain continued till the next morning, when the red god again said that enough had fallen. The black god then turned off the water.

A few days later the black god proposed that they should give the people some more water as the grass was very dry.

The red god, however, was recalcitrant and refused to allow the water to be turned on again.

They disputed for some time, and at length the red god threatened to kill the people, whom he said the black god was spoiling.

At this the black god said: "I shall not allow my people to be killed," and he has been able to protect them, for he lives near at hand, while the red god is above him.

When one hears the thunder crashing in the heavens it is the red god who is trying to come to the earth to kill human beings; and when one hears the distant rumbling, is it the black god who is saying: "Leave them alone, do not kill them."

A Devil

There is a thing which is called a devil. It was formerly a lion, but it changed itself, and one half became a man while the other half became a stone.

This devil can alter its appearance, and is sometimes to be seen one half a lion and the other half a man.

It lives in a forest and is particularly fond of the tree called e-silalei owing to the denseness of its growth.

It only eats human flesh and will not touch wild animals.

When people pass the spot where the devil is, it calls to them, and says: "Come, my brother, help me lift this load of firewood."

If anybody complies with its request, he is struck with the devil's stake, and the devil cries out to him: "I belong to the Aiser clan, escape from me if you can."

When it has spoken thus, it eats the person.

If this devil is known to be in a certain district and people wish to move their kraal, they march all together, and the warriors go in front and behind and on all sides to protect them.

Should a voice be heard issuing from the mist and calling someone, everybody remains silent, for they know that it is this devil that is calling.

The Beginner of the Earth

We were told by the elders that when God came to prepare the world he found three things in the land, a Dorobo, an elephant, and a serpent, all of whom lived together.

After a time the Dorobo obtained a cow.

One day the Dorobo said to the serpent: "Friend, why does my body always itch so that I have to scratch whenever you blow on me?"

The serpent replied: "Oh, my father, I do not blow my bad breath on you on purpose."

At this the Dorobo remained silent, but that same evening he picked up his club, and struck the serpent on the head, and killed it.

On the morrow the elephant asked the Dorobo where the thin one was.

The Dorobo replied that he did not know, but the elephant was aware that he had killed it and that he refused to admit his guilt.

During the night it rained heavily, and the Dorobo was able to take his cow to graze, and he watered it at the puddles of rain.

They remained there many days, and at length the elephant gave birth to a young one.

After a time all the puddles became dry except in one place.

Now the elephant used to go and eat grass, and when she had had enough to eat, she would return to drink at the puddle, lying down in the water and stirring it up so that when the Dorobo drove his cow to water he found it muddy.

One day the Dorobo made an arrow, and shot the elephant, and killed it.

The young elephant then went to another country. "The Dorobo is bad," it said, "I will not stop with him any longer. He first of all killed the snake and now he has killed mother. I will go away and not live with him again."

On its arrival at another country the young elephant met a Masai, who asked it where it came from.

The young elephant replied: "I come from the Dorobo's kraal. He is living in yonder forest and he has killed the serpent and my mother."

The Masai inquired: "Is it true that there is a Dorobo there who has killed your mother and the serpent?"

When he had received a reply in the affirmative, he said: "Let us go there. I should like to see him."

They went and found the Dorobo's hut, which God had turned upside down, and the door of which looked towards the sky.

God then called the Dorobo and said to him: "I wish you to come tomorrow morning for I have something to tell you."

The Masai heard this, and in the morning he went and said to

God: "I have come." God told him to take an axe, and to build a big kraal in three days. When it was ready, he was to go and search for a thin calf, which he would find in the forest. This he was to bring to the kraal and slaughter. The meat was to be tied up in the hide and not to be eaten. The hide was to be fastened outside the door of the hut, firewood was to be fetched, and a big fire lit, into which the meat was to be thrown. He was then to hide himself in the hut, and not to be startled when he heard a great noise outside resembling thunder.

The Masai did as he was bid. He searched for a calf, which he found, and when he had slaughtered it he tied up the flesh in the hide. He fetched some firewood, lit a big fire, threw in the meat, and entered the hut, leaving the fire burning outside.

God then caused a strip of hide to descend from heaven, which was suspended over the calf-skin.

Cattle at once commenced to descend one by one by the strip of hide until the whole of the kraal was filled, when the animals began to press against one another, and to break down the hut where the Masai was.

The Masai was startled, and uttered an exclamation of astonishment. He then went outside the hut, and found that the strip of hide had been cut, after which no more cattle came down from heaven.

God asked him whether the cattle that were there were sufficient, "for," He said, "you will receive no more owing to your being surprised."

The Masai then went away, and attended to the animals which had been given him.

The Dorobo lost the cattle, and has had to shoot game for his food ever since.

Nowadays, if cattle are seen in the possession of Bantu tribes, it is presumed that they have been stolen or found, and the Masai say: "These are our animals, let us go and take them, for God in olden days gave us all the cattle upon the earth."

The Beginner of the Earth (Version 2)

The thing which is called Naiteru-kop is a god, but not as great as the black god.[1]

This is the story which was told us by the elders:

The Masai were formerly Dorobo, and had no cattle: it was the Dorobo who possessed the cattle.

Naiteru-kop came one day and said to a Dorobo: "Come early tomorrow morning, I have something to tell you."

The Dorobo replied: "Very well," and went to sleep.

A Masai named Le-eyo, having heard what had been said to the Dorobo, arose during the night, and waited near the spot where Naiteru-kop was.

When it dawned he went to Naiteru-kop, who said to him: "Who are you?"

On Le-eyo telling him his name, Naiteru-kop asked where the Dorobo was. Le-eyo replied that he did not know.

Naiteru-kop then dropped one end of a piece of hide from the heavens, and let cattle down one by one until the Masai told him to stop.

The Masai cattle wandered off, and as they went the cattle which belonged to the Dorobo mingled with them. The Dorobo were unable to recognize their beasts again, and they lost them.

After this the Dorobo shot away the cord by which the cattle had descended, and God moved and went far off.

When the Dorobo were left without their cattle, they had to shoot wild beasts for their food.

---

[1] Krapf in his *Travels and Missionary Labors in East Africa* writes, "These truculent savages (the Masai and Wakwavi) have a tradition that Engai—heaven or rain—placed a man named Neiterkop on Mount Kenya. He was a kind of demi-god, for he was exalted above men and yet not equal to Engai."

The Story of Le-eyo's Disobedience

One day Naiteru-kop told Le-eyo that if a child were to die he was to say when he threw away the body: "Man, die, and come back again; moon, die, and remain away."

A child died soon afterwards, but it was not one of Le-eyo's, and when he was told to throw it away, he picked it up and said to himself: "This child is not mine; when I throw it away I shall say, 'Man, die, and remain away; moon, die, and return.'"

He threw it away and spoke these words, after which he returned home.

One of his own children died next, and when he threw it away, he said: "Man, die, and return; moon, die, and remain away."

Naiteru-kop said to him: "It is of no use now, for you spoiled matters with the other child."

This is how it came about that when a man dies he does not return, while when the moon is finished, it comes back again and is always visible to us.

The Origin of the Masai and the Bantu People

When Le-eyo grew old, he called his children to him and said to them: "My children, I am now very old, I wish to bid you good-bye."

He then asked his elder son what he wanted out of all his wealth.

His son replied: "I wish something of everything upon the earth."

"Since you want something of everything," the old man said, "take a few head of cattle, a few goats and sheep, and some of the food of the earth, for there will be a large number of things."

The elder son replied: "Very well."

Le-eyo then called his younger son, and asked him what he wanted.

"I should like, Father," the younger one said, "the fan which you carry suspended from your arm."

His father replied: "My child, because you have chosen this fan, God will give you wealth, and you will be great among your brother's people."

The one who selected something of everything became a barbarian, and he who received the fan became the father of all the Masai.

The Story of the Sun and the Moon

We have been told that the sun once married the moon.

One day they fought, and the moon struck the sun on the head; the sun, too, damaged the moon.

When they had done fighting, the sun was ashamed that human beings should see that his face had been battered, so he became dazzlingly bright, and people are unable to regard him without first half closing their eyes.

The moon however is not ashamed, and human beings can look at her face, and see that her mouth is cut and that one of her eyes is missing.

Now the sun and the moon travel in the same direction for many days, the moon leading.

After a time the moon gets tired, and the sun catches her up and carries her.

She is carried thus for two days, and on the third day she is left at the sun's setting place.

At the expiration of these three days, i.e. on the fourth day, the donkeys see the moon reappear, and bray at her.

But it is not until the fifth day that men and cattle see her again.

When a Masai sees the new moon, he throws a twig or stone at it with his left hand, and says, "Give me long life," or "Give me strength"; and when a pregnant woman sees the new moon, she milks some milk into a small gourd which she covers with green grass, and then pours away in the direction of the moon. At the same time she says: "Moon, give me my child safely."

8

The Eclipse of the Moon

When the moon dies (i.e. when there is an eclipse), all the old men and women, the warriors and children come out of their huts and collect together outside. One man then sings in a loud voice deploring the loss of the moon, and everybody present joins in the chorus.

They continue singing in this manner until the moon begins to reappear, when they all shout together as loud as they can:

> "Moon, come to life again!
> Moon, come to life again!"

When they see that the moon has returned to her normal state, they enter their huts and go to sleep.

They do the same thing when there is an eclipse of the sun, the only difference being that when the sun begins to reappear they cry out:

> "Sun, come to life again!
> Sun, come to life again!"

Sunrise and Sunset

If, when the sun rises, the heavens are red, the Masai say it will rain; and if, when the sun sets the sky is the color of blood, they say that there are some warriors out raiding who have been successful.

The Stars

There are three groups of stars with which the Masai are acquainted.

They know whether it will rain or not according to the appearance or nonappearance of the six stars called the Pleiades,[2] which follow after one another like cattle.

When the month which the Masai call Of the Pleiades[3] arrives, and the Pleiades are no longer visible, they know that the rains are over. For the Pleiades set in that month and are not seen again until the season of showers has come to an end:[4] it is then that they reappear.

There are three other stars, which follow one another like the cattle, called the Old Men,[5] and again three others, which pursue them from the left, called the Widows.[6]

Now the Masai say that as the Widows have lost their husbands, they are waylaying the Old Men in order to get married to them.

There is also Kileghen (Venus), and by this planet the Masai know that it is near dawn. It is in consequence also called the Star of the Dawn.

Women pray to Venus when warriors tarry in returning from a raid.

Then there is Leghen (Venus), which when visible is a sign that the moon will shortly rise. Leghen remains in the west, and is only seen in the evening.[7]

---

[2] The Pleiades are seven stars (six of which are visible to the naked eye) situated in the constellation Taurus. They are above the horizon from September till about May 17. The coast people say: "When the Pleiades set in sun (sunny weather), they rise in rain; when they set in rain, they rise in sun."

[3] May.

[4] June–August.

[5] Orion's sword.

[6] Orion's belt.

[7] The Masai have two names for Venus, Kileghen when seen in the morning, and Leghen when seen in the evening (cf. Lucifer and Hesperus, the morning and evening stars of the ancients).

A Halo Round the Moon,
and the Milky Way

If the Masai see a halo round the moon, they say that a place has been attacked and many cattle captured. The halo is supposed to represent the cattle kraal.

Then again, if they see the road which crosses the sky (the Milky Way), they say that this is the road by which the warriors are taking their cattle.

The Rainbow

There is something which the Masai call the rainbow, and if one is seen in the heavens while rain is falling, it is a sign that the rain will shortly cease.

Children call a rainbow "Father's garment" on account of its many colors, one part being red, another white, and a third variegated. They also say: "I will give it to father for he will like it."

Comets

When the Masai see a comet, they know that a great trouble will befall them, the cattle will die, there will be a famine and their people will join the enemies.[8]

It is said that a comet was once seen before the Europeans arrived, and as some Masai children were watering the cattle at a pond after herding them, a creature resembling an ox but green in color issued from the water. The children were frightened, and killed it. They then disemboweled it, and found that its body was full of caul fat instead of blood. On returning to the kraal they related what had occurred.

---

[8] The Dinkas have a similar tradition.

When the medicine men heard the story, he said: "If we see another comet, people who are green in color will come out of the water and visit our country. Should they be killed, caul fat instead of blood will be seen issuing from their bodies."

Shortly after the appearance of the next comet the Europeans arrived. It was formerly believed that they had no blood, and that their bodies were full of caul fat.

Sheet Lightning

If during the months of hunger[9] sheet lighting is seen in the west, the Masai say that there is a big bird of the heavens beating the water with its wings, and that what one sees flashing is the water.

The Story of the Flocks and the Rain and the Sun

When it rains, the goats say: "The enemy have beaten us," and they run away and hide themselves; but the sheep say: "Mother has oiled us," and they remain out in the rain.

When the sun burns fiercely, the sheep say: "The enemy have beaten us," and go and hide themselves in the shade; but the goats say: "Mother has oiled us," and stay in the sun.

The Story of the Night and Day

According to tradition the night is a man and the day his wife.

The origin of this is due to the fact that men, who are strong,

---

[9] September–November.

go and fight the enemy at night time, while women can only work by day.

The Story of the Sky and the Earth

We understand that the sky once married the earth.

As a husband lies on top of his wife in coitus, so the sky lies over the earth. Where the sun shines and the rain falls, the earth receives heat and moisture in just the same way as the woman receives the seed of the man.[10]

Earthquakes

When the Masai feel a shock of earthquake, some say that a number of warriors are going on a raid, others, that a mountain is trembling.[11]

Volcanoes and Steam Jets

If smoke or steam issues from the earth, as for instance at the active volcano Donyo Engai or at the steam jets near the Gilgil river, the Masai say that there is a large deposit of chalk lying beneath the surface and what one sees is dust.

---

[10] [Hollis wrote this passage in Latin, evidently thinking it too racy for his readers.]

[11] When the Bari feel a shock of earthquake they believe that the mountains are fighting (Kaufmann, *Schilderungen*), and the Kéri say that all earthquakes originate from a prominent ridge of hills in their country (*Emin Pasha in Central Africa*).

The Cave in the Mountain of Smoke[12]

There is a cave in the mountain of smoke, or as it is otherwise called Donyo Erok, in which Masai live. If you stand near its mouth you hear the voices of people calling one another and also the lowing of cattle.

Women go to pray at this cave, and take with them gourds full of milk and honey and butter, which they leave there. The inhabitants of the cave come during the night and eat these things.

Barren women, however, do not go to the cave as their offerings are not accepted.

If strangers who do not know about the cave cut a tree near it, blood is seen to issue from the wood.

The Cave of the Athi River and the Lumbwa Masai

There is a cave near the River Athi, which river is called by the Swahili the Hippopotamus River. It is believed that when Naiteru-kop brought the Masai in olden days from the district round about Kenya, and they arrived at Donyo Sabuk, some of them saw this cave and entered it. They journeyed for ten days and eventually reached a salt lake, where they came out of the earth again and settled.

These people are the Lumbwa, who in appearance are like the Masai, but they till the earth.

---

[12] There are numerous traditions connected with the caves which exist in Masailand. The stories here related are examples.

CUSTOMS

Women's Iron Necklaces and
Earrings, and Other Matters

THE REASON WHY women wear necklaces of iron and earrings (called 'surutya) is in order that it shall be known that they are married.

The Masai circumcise girls when they grow up, and these ornaments are worn to make a distinction between girls and women.

For if the women were left without the iron necklaces or the earrings, it could not be ascertained whether they were women or girls.

A Masai girl who has been circumcised is not called girl but woman. That is to say, she is called young woman until she gives birth to a child.

Even if she is very young, she is considered to be grown up as soon as she has been circumcised.

A woman is recognizable by three things, the earrings, the iron necklace, and the big garment, none of which girls possess.

Girls wear beads, small pieces of iron wire (called 'seengani), and other trifles round their necks, and a small cloth. They also have chains in their ears, and armlets and anklets of iron.

They wear one garment and a belt round their waists similar to the warriors.

Women wear nothing round their waists except a broad belt with which they fasten their garments.

They also wear two cloths, one called ol-okesena, and the other ol-lekishopo.

Now with regard to the women's earrings, they are of great

consequence among the Masai, for no woman ventures to leave them off during her husband's lifetime.

Were a woman to take off her earrings and hang them up while doing her work, she would run into her hut on hearing her husband approach, and put them on again, so that he should not see her without them.

If a man goes away from home, his wife does not dare to take off her earrings, for were the other men to see her without them, they would tell her that her husband will hate her.

The Earrings and Arm Rings of Old Men, and Other Matters

Boys and girls put blocks of wood into their ears, called 'n-gulalen,[1] and warriors and old men wear chain earrings, called il-giso.[2] They also have chain bracelets.

No Masai elder may wear the earrings called 'surutya unless he has children who have been circumcised and become warriors and women; but he who has grown up children may wear 'surutya.

There is another thing, an arm ring called ol-masangus, which is cut out of a buffalo horn or an elephant's tusk, and made to look beautiful.

No elder may wear this unless he has large herds of cattle and many children.

He who is well known to possess many head of cattle and also many children may wear this arm ring as a sign of his wealth.

---

[1] These blocks are gradually increased in size as the lobe stretches. The proper length is attained if the lobes meet at the top of the head. Perhaps the largest Masai earring in existence is one of stone weighing 2 lb. 14 oz., which the author recently presented to the British Museum.

[2] The same word is used for rings which young men, women, and children wear. They are made of iron or brass wire, and are frequently worn on the thumb as well as on the four fingers.

There is also an arm clamp called e-rap, which the warriors wear, but they only put this on as an ornament.

Salutations

When one warrior meets another, he says: "Sopai"; and when several warriors meet, one party says: "Endasopai, O warriors!" The reply to these greetings is "Hepa."

Then, if it is desired to ask the news of the country from whence the people come, they are asked: "Do you bring good tidings?" or "Do you relate good news?"

They reply: "Only the things which are good," or simply, "Good news only."

When Masai warriors meet old men, the latter start the greetings. If there are many warriors, the old men call to them and say: "Friends."

To this the warriors reply: "Yes."

The elders then say: "Endasopai."

And the warriors answer all together: "Hepa."

When warriors come from a distant country and see some elders outside a kraal, they go up to them, and take their hands, at the same time thrusting their spears into the earth. The elders then say to them: "Greeting."

When they have dropped one another's hands, the elders say to the warriors: "Friends," and the warriors answer: "Yes." The elders then give the usual salutation: "Endasopai," to which the warriors reply all together: "Hepa."

Nowadays, however, the warriors do not wait to be greeted by the elders, and call out "Endasopai, O ye fathers!" At any rate the so-called El-burgon Masai do this. When the warriors of the Kisongo Masai greet the elders first, they say: "Endasopai, O elders!" or "Endasopai, O old people!"

When old people meet one another, they say: "Endasopai, O ye elders!" or "Endasopai, O ye husbands!"

No warrior or boy would dare to say: "Endasopai, O husbands!" for he would be told he is wanting in respect.

When warriors meet married women, they say: "Endakwenya, O old ladies!" to which the women reply, "Igho."

No warriors would dare to say to married women: "Endakwenya, O wives!" for it would be said that he was wanting in respect.

It is only the old men who may say to their wives: "Endakwenya, O wives!"

When married women greet warriors or boys, they say: "Endakwenya, O children!" And the warrior or boy replies: "Igho."

When warriors greet married women of their own clan, they say: "Endakwenya, O great ladies!"

To this the women reply: "Igho."

Warriors greet girls by saying: "Endasopai, O girls!"

The girls reply, "Hepa."

The same words are spoken when girls greet warriors.

A girl does not say "Sopai," to her brother, nor does a warrior greet his sister in this fashion: they say "Takwenya." Some also kiss one another.

A warrior might, however, say "Sopai" to his sister if she is quite young.

When small children or even big boys greet their elders, they do not take their hands, but they butt them with their heads, striking the old people with their foreheads in the pit of the stomach.

If a woman kisses a small child, the latter touches her breast with its face. The woman then says: "Greeting."

Departure

If a Masai has paid a visit to some friends, and wishes to return home, he ties up his things.

When he is ready, he says: "Well, I am about to go."

The owners of the kraal reply: "All right! Good-bye. Pray to God, accost only the things which are safe, and meet nobody but blind people."

The guest then says: "Lie down with honey wine and milk," to which the owners of the kraal reply: "So be it."

After this the stranger is at liberty to depart to his own country.

Hospitality

When a Masai goes to other kraals to pay a visit, he does not on his arrival enter a hut unless he knows the owner, for if he belongs, for instance, to the Aimer age, he must not enter the hut of one of the Kishumu age, as he does not belong to this age.

He will ask where the huts of the members of the Aimer age are, and when he has been shown them, he will enter one.

When he has entered, the owner of the hut leaves him and goes to search for a place to sleep in elsewhere, the stranger remaining with his wife.[3]

Or if the owner of the hut has several wives, he goes to sleep with one of these, leaving the stranger in the hut he entered.

A Masai cannot refuse hospitality to a stranger (of his own age) for he is afraid that the other members of his age will curse him, and he will die.

Cattle, Grass, and Milk

The Masai love their cattle very much, and consider that nothing in the world is of equal value.[4] As with people, each cow is known by name.

There is a saying which is as follows:

"One cow resembles a man's head."

They mean by this that if a man has a cow, which he looks after and tends, it bears, and by so doing enables him to live, for he can marry, and have children, and thus become rich.

Now cattle feed on grass, and the Masai love grass on this account.

---

[3] See footnote 27, page 84.

[4] The Masai cattle are of the humped Zebu type. Schweinfurth (*The Heart of Africa*) writes with regard to the Dinka and other Nilotic tribes: "The poor savages . . . pay almost a divine homage to their cattle which they hold dearer than wife or child." Kaufmann (*Schilderungen*) adds that on the death of a cow a Dinka goes into mourning as he would if a relation had died.

Whenever there is a drought, the women fasten grass onto their clothes, and go and offer up prayers to God.

If a warrior beats a boy on the grazing ground, the boy tears up some grass, and when the warrior sees that the child has grass in his hand, he stops beating him.

Again, if the Masai fight with an enemy, and wish to make peace, they hold out some grass as a sign.

Whenever warriors return from a raid, and it is desired to praise those who have killed some of the enemy, a girl takes a small gourd of milk, and having covered it with green grass, sprinkles it over them.

Then, if people move from one kraal to another, they tie grass onto the gourds.

Should one man ask forgiveness of another with grass in his hand and his request be not attended to, it is said that the man who refuses to listen to his prayer is a Dorobo, and that he does not know about cattle.

Again, if a man who is proceeding on a journey sees a tree which has fallen on the road, he pulls up some grass, and throws it on the tree; otherwise he fears that his journey will not be successful.

The Masai love grass very much, for they say: "God gave us cattle and grass, we do not separate the things which God has given us."

Whenever Masai women milk their cows, they take some milk from the gourd and pour it away, for they say: "God likes this."

The Brand Marks and Ear Cutting of Cattle, Sheep, and Donkeys

The brand marks which the Masai use for their cattle are not alike.

For each clan and family there is one principal mark, and all the cattle belonging to the various members of a family are branded in a special way.

There are also small marks by which the actual owner can be recognized.

Besides branding, each family has a special method of slitting the ears of their cattle, sheep, and donkeys.

They likewise have smaller marks for each individual owner.

If therefore a cow is seen, it can be recognized as belonging to the Aiser clan, for instance, and also to such and such a person.

Warriors' Shields and Spears

The warriors' shields are not all of one design; they differ.

Each age and each subdistrict has its own design.

In consequence, if the warriors meet an enemy, it is known to what age such a one belongs, and also to what subdistrict.

There are four markings for the shields, the red one, the black one, the ornamental one, and the one for bravery.[5]

Likewise with the spears, they are not all marked alike.

If a spear is found, it can be ascertained by looking at the lower part to what age and also to what subdistrict its owner belongs.

Arrows of the Elders

The old men have special marks for their arrows as the warriors have for their spears.

If an arrow is found, the generation and the subdistrict to which its owner belongs can be recognized.

---

[5] The Masai make use of four colors in ornamenting their shields—white, red, black, and gray. White is obtained by mixing water with white clay; red clay mixed with the juice of the *Solanum campylacanthum* produces the red paint; black is procured from the ashes of *Mœrua uniflora,* or from charred potsherds and gourds; and gray, which is but rarely used, is obtained from cinders.

The Process of Moving

The Masai are fond of moving, and if they happen to be staying in a place where the grazing is poor, they move to another spot.

When they move, they saddle their donkeys with skins and pack-saddles in which they put their gourds, and the women carry bags.

Should they stop in a place where the grass is not good, they do not build proper huts, but they live in the so-called il-ngobori, i.e. in huts made of skins. When they go to a good grazing ground they build huts.

The women do the work of building. They procure poles, and put one end in holes, which they dig in the ground; they then bind the poles together with cord made from trees; after which they cover the framework with long grass. When they have finished this, they plaster the whole of the outside with cow dung and mud.

Warriors' Kraals and Slaughterhouses

Masai warriors do not live in the kraals of the married people; they have their own kraals, where they dwell with their mothers and lovers.

When they go to the woods to eat meat, they live in the slaughterhouses[6] with their boy servants.

The Feast Called the Offspring

There is a feast known to the Masai as the Offspring.

When a child is born, and the time has arrived for it to be

---

[6] Meat may not be eaten in the manyat, or warriors' kraals, and special places, called il-puli, are erected in the woods, to which the warriors retire when they slaughter cattle.

given a name, a bullock is slaughtered which is called The (Bullock) of the Offspring.

A black bullock, and one without a blemish or a white or brown spot on it, is selected, and slaughtered.

The meat is then divided up between the women and men.[7]

When the meat has been cooked and is nearly ready, one woman stands up and calls the others. She cries out as follows: "The honey is ready, this is for the first time; the honey is ready, this is for the second time; the meat is ready, this is for the first time; the meat is ready, this is for the second time."

The women of the kraal then carry milk to the child's mother, and after each has been given her share of the meat, they take their departure.

In the evening the mother carries her child to the cattle kraal, and milks the cows with the child on her back.

When she has finished, three old men and the child's father (which makes four) join her, and the child is named.

The so-called offspring bullock is always slaughtered at the door of the hut, and the skull, instead of being thrown away, is placed by the door. The tail is not separated from the hide as is usually the case: it is left on until the hide is worn out.

Now the offspring bullock is not of necessity slaughtered when the child is born; it is permissible to wait until he is big and until he is about to be circumcised. No person is circumcised, however, until this bullock has been slaughtered.

Circumcision

The following is a Masai custom:

A Masai child cannot be circumcised until the father has observed a custom called The passing of the fence.

The man who wishes to have his eldest child circumcised

---

[7] Men and women never eat their meals together.

brews some honey wine, and calls his neighbors together while it is being prepared.

A hut is then built for him outside the kraal, and he stays there for four days alone. He also sleeps there, and his food is taken to him.

During these four days he only approaches the kraal to look after his cattle when they are grazing outside.

He must don the clothes, ornaments, and weapons of a warrior—the sword, the spear, the club, and the shield, the cap made from the stomach of a goat, the headdress of ostrich feathers,[8] and the cape of vultures' feathers, the anklets of colobus-monkey skin, the arm clamp, the garment of calfskin, and the piece of goat's skin fastened to the waist.

When the four days have elapsed, some of the elders go and bring him back to the kraal.

He has to stand by the door of the hut where the honey wine, which has previously been prepared, is kept.

One elder then says to him who is passing the fence: "Go, become an old man."

The latter replies: "Ho! I shall not . . . !"

The order is repeated, but he still refuses.

On being told for the fifth time, he says: "Ho! I have gone then."

He then enters the hut and puts aside the warrior's paraphernalia; the honey wine is drunk; and he is called by his son's name, thus: The father of so-and-so.

When he replies to this name, he is told to go and make a profit. He answers: "Herds and flocks."

This is repeated four times, and the ceremony is over.

After this any of his children, whether girls or boys, may be circumcised.

---

[8] Sometimes instead of the ostrich-feather headdress one made of lion's or leopard's skin is worn, and occasionally the headdress called ol-marangash is substituted. This headdress is worn by the warriors when they slaughter cattle in the woods.

Boys' Circumcision

When Masai boys wish to be circumcised—having previously ascertained that the time for circumcision has arrived—all those who live in neighboring districts collect together, and, taking cattle and honey with them, go to the medicine man's kraal.

The only weapons which they may carry in their hands are sticks; they have neither spears nor swords, and their clubs are stuck into their belts.

Those who come from countries far off, such as Kiteto or Moipo, or other distant places, may take their bows, but they must leave their arrows and quivers behind.

When they have received permission to hold the circumcision festival, they enjoy themselves, and paint their bodies with chalk.

They then pay visits to different kraals during the next two or three months, after which they return home, where they remain until they are circumcised.[9]

When a Masai boy is circumcised, the ceremony is started by his being shaved, after which a sheep or bullock is slaughtered, which is called The (animal) that has caused him to be taken out (from the boys' ranks).

On the second day the boy sallies forth to cut a tree called El-latim, which is carried by girls to the kraal, where it is planted at the door of the hut.

The next morning the boy goes and sits down outside the kraal to get cold. He also washes himself with water in which a fern called Father's spear[10] has been soaked.

When the sun is some way above the horizon, his mother opens the gate of the kraal, and fetches an oxhide which she puts on the ground by the right-hand doorpost.

The boy then takes his place on the hide, and the operator, a

---

[9] It is at this time that the boys of each subdistrict choose one of their number to be their ol-aigwenani, that is to say, their counselor or spokesman, who is also their judge and their representative at the chief medicine man's court.

[10] *Asparagus* sp.

Dorobo, comes together with the men whose duty it is to hold the boy.

The man who holds him straightens out his legs, and the boy sits between them and is circumcised.

If the boy winces during the operation, his mother is beaten with sticks; and if the boy's parents know that he will behave like a coward, they go away and hide themselves.

As soon as the operation is over, the hide on which is the blood is carried by the boy and placed on his bed.

When the boys have all been circumcised they are called Sipolio (recluse).

They remain at home for four days, and bows are prepared for them.

They then sally forth and shoot at the young girls, their arrows being blocked with a piece of honey-comb so that they cannot penetrate into the girls' bodies.

They also shoot small birds,[11] which they wear round their heads together with ostrich feathers.

The Sipolio like to appear as women and wear the surutya earrings and garments reaching to the ground. They also paint their faces with chalk.

When they have all recovered, they are shaved again and become Il-barnot (the shaved ones). They then discard the long garments and wear warriors' skins and ornaments.

After this their hair is allowed to grow, and as soon as it has grown long enough to plait, they are called Il-muran (warriors).

The warriors are fond of the titles 'L-oingok (the bulls) and 'N-gaminini (the generous people), for they may then wear bells or a bracelet called il-torongen.

Now to become one of the Oingok, a warrior must kill many savages, while the Gaminini are chosen if they frequently slaughter bullocks and give the meat to their comrades.

---

[11] The bird which the Sipolio wear round their heads is the mouse bird (*Colius affinis*). Boys who behaved in a cowardly manner during the operation are not allowed to shoot these birds.

Girls' Circumcision

When Masai girls wish to marry, they are circumcised.

On the day that the operation is performed, a sheep or bullock is slaughtered, and as with the boys it is called The (animal) which has caused her to be taken out (from among the girls).

Women are operated upon indoors, and it is not considered a disgrace if they cry out.

Instead of the ostrich feathers which the boys wear, a wreath made from the leaves of the *Hyphaene* (or doum) palm, or of grass, is donned.

When they recover, they are married.

The Feast Called E-unoto
or the Selection of a Chief[12]

If the warriors wish to select a chief, who is called Ol-aunoni, they choose a man whose parents are still living, who owns cattle and has never killed anybody, whose parents are not blind, and who himself has not a discolored eye.

When they succeed in getting such a one, they do not inform him; it is kept hidden from him until the time for the celebration of the feast arrives.

If the chief medicine man approves of the selection, a cloth is made for the new chief like those worn by the old men, and surutya earrings are obtained.

Just before the feast a small kraal, called O-singira, is built a short distance from the warriors' kraal.

Only milk cows are placed in this kraal.

---

[12] A chief called Ol-aunoni is appointed for each subdistrict. His duties are to keep the warriors of his subdistrict together, and he is responsible to the chief medicine man for their appearance in case of war. If a warrior disobeys the orders of his chief, he is flogged or maltreated by his companions.

On the day of the feast the chief is seized, for if he were told that he is to be chosen, he would run away and hide, or kill someone. The idea of becoming an old man is distasteful to him, since he will be unable to again go to the wars.

When he has been seized, the surutya earrings are put on him, and he is clothed like an old man. After this the work for the day is over.

On the morrow a black bullock with a white neck and belly is sought out from the herds, and surrounded by the warriors.

When the cattle go to the grazing ground, a strong man is chosen, who holds the bullock by the horn at arm's length, while another one seizes it by the navel.

The bullock is stabbed in the nape of the neck,[13] and skinned on the spot.

The old men then light a big fire in the center of the warriors' kraal, and throw a buffalo horn into it.

When the fire is dying down, the warriors standing outside are called, and told that, "it is finished."

They all run towards the spot, racing to get the horn.

The one who arrives first puts his hand in the fire, and, taking out the horn, stretches out his arm. He shows it to the others, and cries out: "I have finished it."

With this the E-unoto feast terminates.

The Aunoni, or chief, is shaved on the same day together with the Aigwenani, or Counselor, who was elected before the feast of circumcision.

Afterwards the warriors may be shaved whenever they wish.

When the warriors have elected their chief, they slaughter cattle, and wait for four or five months, at the expiration of which they proceed on a raid. This is called The (fulfillment) of the vow *or* The (selection) of the chief.

---

[13] All the Nilotic tribes butcher their cattle by stabbing them in the nape of the neck (Schweinfurth, *The Heart of Africa*).

They wear cotton cloths,[14] called The vow,[15] on which are sewn the seeds of the ekirikiti tree.[16]

They also wear necklaces made of twigs of the e-syaïti tree,[17] and called Mangäk, and some carry their fathers' snuff boxes or fans with them.

Marriage[18]

When a Masai wishes to marry, he commences his courtship by making love to a girl while she is still young, and by presenting some tobacco to her father.

He then waits until the girl grows up, when he again offers presents of honey and tobacco.

More honey is given to the father at his daughter's circumcision.

On the young woman's recovery the man proceeds to his future father-in-law's kraal, and takes with him the dowry, viz. three heifers and two bullocks, one of the latter being said to keep the heifers company, while the other is slaughtered at the door of the hut. His sister also takes a pot of honey and accompanies him.

The bullock which accompanies the heifers is given to the bride's father in order that the two men may call one another Pakiteng, i.e. the giver and receiver of a bullock, or father and son-in-law.

When the time arrives for the husband to fetch his wife, he takes

---

[14] Before cotton cloths were introduced, dressed skins sewn together were worn. 'N-dorosi garments are worn like the Spanish poncho, a slit being made in the middle for the head to pass through.

[15] A raid undertaken after a long peace is spoken of by the same word. Any warrior who shirks his duties on an occasion of this sort can be put to death, and his murderer will not be punished.

[16] *Erythrina tomentosa.*

[17] *Acalypha fruticosa.*

[18] Formerly no Masai was able to marry until he had been on several raids, but nowadays they leave the ranks of the warriors (il-muran) and settle down as married men (il-móruak) at a comparatively early age.

with him three sheep (two rams and a young ewe). The ewe he presents to the mother to enable them to call one another Pakerr, i.e. the giver and receiver of a sheep, or mother and son-in-law.

The two rams are slaughtered together with two others, which the girl's father provides.

After the bride's wedding garments have been oiled, she puts them on, and is given a gourd which has been ornamented with cowries. This is put on her back, and she is taken by her husband, who is accompanied by two of his friends and two of the old women from his bride's kraal, to her future home.

She does not hurry but walks very slowly until she reaches her husband's kraal, where a child is given her to feed.

When a man marries, it is considered unlucky if he calls his wife by her name. He must give her another name. A favorite method is to call her by the age to which she belongs, thus, The (woman) of the Seure age.

If a Masai owns large herds of cattle he is able to marry many wives. Some have two wives, others three, and others four; while if rich men wish, they may have as many as ten or twenty.

When a Masai marries for the second or third time, his first wife gives the new wife a calf, after which they call one another Paashe, i.e. the giver and receiver of a calf.

No Masai may marry a woman belonging to the same subdivision as himself if both families live in the same district, but he may marry a woman of his own clan or one belonging to another clan.

The Refuge[19]

If the Masai men beat their wives, some go and seek refuge elsewhere, while others suffer and stop at home.

Should a husband beat his wife, but not badly, she will seek refuge in the house of a member of her husband's age.

---

[19] Divorce appears to be unknown among the Masai.

When the man with whom she has taken refuge returns her to her owner, the latter does not beat her again, for he fears that he will be cursed by the members of his age.

If a woman commits a serious crime, and knows that she will be beaten in consequence, she goes to her father's kraal, and is given an ox, which she takes to her husband and begs forgiveness.

Death

On the death of a child, or a warrior, or a woman among the Masai, the body is thrown away,[20] and the person's name is buried, i.e. it is never again mentioned by the family.

Should there be anything which is called by that name, it is given another name which is not like that of the deceased.

For instance, if an unimportant person called Ol-onana (he who is soft, or weak, or gentle) were to die, gentleness would not be called en-nanai in that kraal, as it is the name of a corpse, but it would be called by another name, such as epolpol (it is smooth).

And if anybody of that kraal were to ask for news of the great medicine man Ol-onana, he would call him Ol-opolpol.

If an elder dies leaving children, his name is not buried, for his descendants are named after him.

When old men or women die, they are not wept for, nor are they thrown away like others who die young.

New sandals are made, a sheep is slaughtered, the fat is roasted, and the body anointed.

After this the corpse is carried to a shady place, where a bullock is slaughtered, and all the meat is eaten on the spot. The

---

[20] The body is always taken to the west of the kraal, towards the setting sun. It is laid on the left side with the head towards the north, so that the face looks towards the east. The legs are drawn up to the chest, the left hand supports the head, and the right arm is folded across the breast.

bones of the bullock are left with the body so that the hyenas may smell it, and come and carry it away, and devour it.

On the death of a Masai medicine man or rich person the corpse is not thrown away. An ox or a sheep is slaughtered, and the fat is taken and rubbed on the body, after which it is put in an ox-hide and carried to a shady spot. A small hole is then dug resembling a trench, into which the body is laid and covered with stones. This is called a grave. Whenever anybody passes this spot he throws a stone on to the heap, and this is done for all time.

If a Masai woman gives birth to a boy after the death of one of her sons, a small piece is cut off the ear of the newly born babe and he is called Nawaya, i.e. from whom it has been snatched.

When the child grows up his name is changed to Ol-awara, which has the same meaning.

Sometimes children's ears are not cut, in which case they wear a special kind of bracelet, called En-daret, and a ring on one of their toes.[21]

Mourning

When a father of a family dies, the whole family mourns for him.

His widows lay aside their earrings, necklaces, and beads; his daughters leave off their chains, beads, armlets, and anklets; and his warrior sons and boys shave their heads.

His wives wait for a whole year before they put on their ornaments again.

If any other person dies, the women of the family leave off their small neck ornaments but not the iron rings or the earrings, and the men shave their heads. The mourning lasts for one month.

If a baby dies, its mother only lays aside her ornaments.

---

[21] The second toe of the right foot.

People's Souls and Spirits, and Snakes

When a man is on the point of death, people say he is about to cut his heart; and when he dies and is eaten (by hyenas), his soul dies with him. It is believed that all is over as with the cattle, and that the soul does not come to life again.

But when a medicine man or a rich person dies and is buried, his soul turns into a snake as soon as his body rots; and the snake goes to his children's kraal to look after them.[22]

The Masai in consequence do not kill their sacred snakes, and if a woman sees one in her hut, she pours some milk on the ground for it to lick, after which it will go away.

There is a black snake, which is sacred to the Aiser clan; and if a person of another clan were to strike the snake while the owners were present, they would tell him to desist as it belongs to them.

The Tarosero family have their own particular snakes, which are of many hues; and when a member of this family fights with someone and gets the worst of the combat, he calls upon his snakes, and says: "The avengers of my mother's house, come out!" If the man with whom he is fighting does not run away, the snakes will come and bite him.

The other clans and families have their sacred snakes as well. Some are white in color, others red, and others green. Some have a hood like an old man's cloak, others again have white heads like very old people.

The medicine men are also said to have snakes, which they keep in their bags.

It is believed that the souls of some big people like Mbatian[23] go to heaven after death and burial.

---

[22] The Dinka, Bari, Latuka, and other Nilotic tribes also pay reverence to snakes. The Zulus hold that divine ancestral shades are embodied in certain tame and harmless snakes, whom their human kinsfolk receive with kindly respect and propitiate with food.

[23] See pages 93–95 below.

A sleeping man must not be awakened suddenly. He must be roused gently, for it is thought that his soul may perhaps not return and he will die.

The Masai say there are no such things as ghosts because they do not see them. But it is supposed that cattle see them, and when a herd of cattle all gaze at one spot, they are said to be looking at either a ghost or a beast of prey.

Inheritance

When the father of a family dies, his eldest son inherits all his property,[24] and also the herds and flocks belonging to the childless widows, but not those which are the property of widows who have sons.

The sons by each wife inherit the cattle belonging to their mother's family.

If a man dies childless, his brothers inherit his cattle and his half-brothers his wives. It is unlawful for a man's own brothers (i.e. brothers by the same mother) to take his wives.

Should a widow have a son by her late husband's half-brother or by another man, the child is given the cattle which he would otherwise have inherited had his mother's former husband been alive, and he is considered to belong to that family.

If a man dies and leaves a son who is a minor, the property which he inherits is taken care of for him until he grows up.[25]

It is considered unlawful for a man to inherit the property of his maternal uncle.

---

[24] The Masai distribute their herds and flocks among their wives during their lifetime, each one being given a certain number to look after and milk. The cattle so distributed are said to belong to the wife's family, and are recognized as the property of her sons, who, however, do not assume ownership until after their father's death.

[25] In a case of this kind, the child does not go to the wars, but marries soon after he is circumcised.

Theft

If a Masai steals milk, or meat, or other small things, he is not fined.

Grown-up people, however, rarely steal, it is the boys who take the milk and meat, etc.

While the Masai do not consider it wrong to steal trifles of this nature, they dislike immensely having their cattle stolen.

Should any warriors steal an ox and be caught by the owner, they would have to pay; and if three men took part in the theft, each would have to pay three heifers.

In the event of the owner following up the thieves and catching them in the act of slaughtering the stolen animal, one of the warriors might see him and call out "Guilty," in which case he would not be fined heavily. While the others would be fined in heifers, he who had cried "Guilty" would only have to pay a young bull. Were all of them to cry "Guilty," they would all be fined in young bulls.

Seduction

If a warrior causes a woman to conceive, he marries her.

When a warrior loves a woman very much, he purposely seduces her to enable him to take her as wife.

But the Masai consider it wrong for unmarried people to have children, and if you say to a girl: "Go away, you who have conceived," she will weep bitterly.

A child not born in wedlock is called The child of seduction or The child of the fireplace.

Murder

If a Masai warrior strikes another and kills him, he runs away and hides himself.

Should there be no judges, the brothers of the murdered man will kill the murderer.

If the latter is not killed, the elders make peace between the two families, and garments are exchanged. The family of the murdered man takes the murderer's garment, and the latter takes the garment of one of the dead man's brothers.

The murdered man's brothers then wait for two years, at the expiration of which they call together all their clan, and go and lift the murderer's cattle, taking them as they would in a raid.

If there is a cow in the herd with a bell tied round its neck, it is left behind.

The herdsman is carried off as well; but when the party have arrived at the kraal where the murdered man lived, he is allowed to return to his own kraal.

Blood money is not paid by the Masai until two years have elapsed, for they say that the dead man's head is still fresh.[26]

When one Masai kills another, it is called committing murder, it is not called killing. Killing is only used when referring to savages.

If a warrior strikes another and tears the lobe of his ear, he has to pay a young ewe. If he breaks a bone, either in his leg, arm, or head, he has to pay a heifer.

If a boy is murdered, the amount which has to be paid is not as great as for a warrior, the price being fifty young bulls.

Adultery

No warrior or boy may commit adultery with a woman of his father's age. If he does so, and it becomes known, he is cursed.

Should he be cursed, he pays two oxen (one in lieu of honey wine), and he prays the elders to remove the curse. The elders eat the ox when they drink their honey wine.

---

[26] This law is not always put into force. The murdered man's relations are often willing to make peace on payment of a heavy fine, say 100 head of cattle.

But this is not the case if a man commits adultery or fornication with a woman or girl of his own age. This is not an offense.[27]

If an old man commits adultery with his daughter or with a girl of her age, it is considered a serious crime. The other old men if they hear of it beat him, pull down his kraal, and slaughter whichever of his cattle they want.

The Extraction of Teeth

There is something called em-bwata, which means the extracting of the two middle incisors of the lower jaw.

A knife is used with which to perform the operation.

The Masai extract their children's two middle teeth twice. They extract them first of all when the child is about eight months old, and all its teeth have grown. Then they wait.

After the child has lost all its milk teeth and obtained the permanent set, i.e. when it is about twelve years old, the teeth are extracted a second time, and never grow again.

When a child has had its teeth extracted, donkey's dung is put on its face in order to cool it.

The origin of this custom of extracting teeth was to enable people, in the event of a man falling ill or being on the point of death, when his teeth would pain him, to pour water through the orifice.[28]

---

[27] From this it will be seen that the Masai are polyandrous as well as polygamous. A man may marry as many wives as he can afford to purchase, and a woman may cohabit with any man belonging to her husband's age.

[28] Hinde (*The Last of the Masai*) writes: "The origin of this custom is supposed to date back to a time when tetanus was a great scourge among the Masai, and they discovered that it was a comparatively simple matter to feed a man suffering from lockjaw if two of his front teeth were missing." Sir H. Johnston, in commenting upon this, says (*The Uganda Protectorate*, p. 803): "It may be this explanation has been invented recently to explain a very ancient custom inherited by the Masai from the Nilotic stock, which was their origin; for among these people the removal of the lower incisor teeth is a very common practice." Hinde's explanation, however, appears to be very widely spread.

Had people formerly extracted the upper teeth, they would not have required the hole in the lower jaw. But now they have become accustomed to the latter.

When the Masai see a man who has not had the two middle incisors extracted, they laugh at him, and say: "He eats his food like a donkey."

Shaving

Masai elders, women,[29] and children shave their heads and eyebrows, and pull out their eyelashes if they enter their eyes.

They also pull out or shave the hairs of the beard, armpits, and pubes, and some singe the hairs of their shins.

If warriors are not in mourning,[30] they may not shave their heads until they have held the feast called e-unoto,[31] and they grow pigtails.

When a woman gives birth to a child, neither she nor the child are shaved until the latter has four teeth, two in the upper jaw and two in the lower.

The hair of the head is called the mane.

Spitting

The Masai have two ways of spitting; one is used to show contempt, and the other astonishment. Besides this the medicine men spit when they wish to heal people.[32]

---

[29] This very uncommon practice for women to shave their heads is also followed by the Dinkas, Baris, and Latukas (Cummins, "Sub-Tribes of the Bahr-el-Ghazal Dinkas," *Journal of the Anthropological Institute,* June, 1904; and Baker, *The Albert Nyanza.*).

[30] See "Mourning," page 79 above.

[31] See above, p. 74 ff.

[32] Among the Dinkas it is also customary for the medicine men to spit on their patients (Kaufmann, *Schilderungen*).

If a Masai wishes to show his contempt for another man, he expectorates a small stream of saliva forcibly through the hole in his teeth into the man's face, and says at the same time: "You are a dog."

Formerly when the Masai saw Swahilis, they used to spit on the ground and say: "These coast people stink like fowls." They never went near them or touched them if they could help it.

When a Masai sees a baby that he has never seen before, he spits on it slightly several times and says: "Grow, become accustomed to the eyes of people."

When he sees a child that he has never before beheld, he also spits on it slightly, and says: "This child is bad." To himself, however, he says: "This child is good." It is believed that if he praises a child it will fall ill.

If small children salute very old men,[33] the latter spit on them, and say: "May God give you long life and gray hairs like mine."[34]

Then, when warriors greet old men,[35] the latter frequently spit in their hands before allowing the young men to grasp them.

If a Masai sees something phenomenal, such as a shooting star, he spits several times and says: "Be lost! go in the direction of the enemy!" after which he says: "Stay away from me."

Again, should he forget, and call somebody who is dead, or mention the name of a deceased person, he spits. Should he hear any bad news, such as the death of some person, he spits, and says: "Be lost, O God, we have no ears."

When the Europeans came to these countries and the Masai saw them for the first time, they used to spit, for they said: "We have never seen people like these." They also called them medicine men, and if a European gave a Masai medicine, the latter asked him to spit on him to heal him. Europeans were formerly called 'L-Ojuju owing to their being hairy.

---

[33] See page 65 above.

[34] It is customary among the Bari people for old men (fathers or grandfathers) to take children's heads between their knees and spit slightly on them to bless them.

[35] See page 64 above.

Food

Among the Masai the principal food of the old men, the women, and the children is milk.

The warriors alone drive bullocks into the forest, and slaughter them there: at other times they go to the married people's kraals and drink milk, but they never remain for two months together without slaughtering.

Whenever the old men, the women, and the boys are able to do so, they likewise eat meat. They also eat an ox if it dies a natural death,[36] or if it is bitten by a snake, or if a beast of prey has killed it.

The Masai elders, however, do not slaughter their cattle without good cause, and a man who is very fond of meat is called a Dorobo.

Whenever a woman gives birth to a child, a bullock is slaughtered, and she is given the fat.

A pregnant woman is not given good food. When she wants meat, she is given bones or lean scraps; and when she wants milk, water is mixed with it.

The Masai are also very fond of blood. They tie a leather ligature round the neck of a beast and pierce a vein with an arrow, the shaft of which has been blocked. When the blood gushes forth, they catch it in gourds. Some drink it pure; others mix it with milk.

There are a few other things which the Masai eat.

Some old men and women chew tobacco mixed with salt and *Ocimum suave,* while others sniff ground tobacco up their nostrils: this latter is called snuff. Others again smoke pipes.

Those of the warriors who like it also take snuff. The boys and girls, however, neither take snuff nor chew tobacco.[37]

The Masai do not grow tobacco themselves, for they do not

---

[36] The Shiluk and other Nilotic tribes also eat cattle which have died a natural death.

[37] In olden days it was the privilege of rich old men and their chief wives only to take tobacco, which was called ol-chani loo-'ng-onyek, the eye-medicine.

88 A. C. Hollis

know how to dig. They buy it from savages, exchanging it for butter and lean goats.

The Masai do not sell good cattle to the savages; they only give them barren cows, or those which have no milk, or which do not care for their calves. These and old or lean goats and sheep are the only animals they part with.

The old men drink honey wine, and they purchase from the savages two kinds of beer, called Ol-marua and En-joi.

It is only the children who like wild honey: old men eat the comb full of grubs.[38]

Children are very fond of various kinds of fruit, which are also eaten by the old people, but the latter do not care for them very much.

Formerly the Masai, when they had plenty of cattle, ate no other kind of food, but nowadays they often have to eat savages' food, such as maize, rice, bananas, and cereals, for they no longer own the vast herds which they formerly possessed.

They, however, do not eat everything. They eat neither birds, nor fish, nor the flesh of wild animals.

Wild Animals

The Masai ate the flesh of no wild animals when in olden days they all had cattle; but some of those who have lost all their cattle are now beginning to eat venison, like the Dorobo.

If Masai boys kill elephants, they only take the tusks, which they exchange for cattle.

When buffaloes are killed, the hide and the horns are kept. From the former the warriors make their shields, and from the latter mortars are cut in which medicines are ground. The medicine men also use the horns to put stones in for their prophecies.

If a giraffe is killed, only the long hairs of the tail are preserved. The girls use these as thread to sew the beads onto their clothes.

---

[38] The Masai obtain their honey by following the *Cuculus indicator* bird.

Should an eland be killed, strips of the hide are taken and made into thongs for fastening the cattle with.

When an ostrich is killed, the feathers are made into head-dresses, which are worn by the warriors when they go to war. Boys also wear ostrich feathers when they are circumcised.

Whenever a lion is killed, the hide is taken, and the warriors make a headdress out of the mane. They wear this when they go to war.

If a wildebeest is killed, the tail is kept, and the elders make their fans from it.

Should a greater kudu be killed, the horns are preserved and blown when people move their kraals, so that nobody shall lose the way.

Lastly, if a rhinoceros is killed, its horn is taken and carved into clubs, which are used for beating the he-goats and bulls with. The counselors' clubs are also made of rhinoceros horn.

These are the wild animals of which the Masai make use.

A Masai will also kill a beast of prey if he sees it eating cattle or goats, for he says: "It has eaten our cattle." The beasts of prey which eat cattle and goats are lions, leopards, hyenas, and jackals.

Games

Small Masai children collect pebbles or berries, with which they play at cattle and sheep. They also build huts and kraals in the sand, and they make spears out of bulrushes. Little girls make dolls of the fruit of the sausage-tree.[39]

Big boys play about in the herds of cattle. They choose a quiet animal, and pretend it is a hut. One boy stands by the cow while the others go and hide. When the latter return, the one who is standing by the cow chases them away. If one of the boys who is driven off is caught, they say the enemy have killed him; anybody who manages to escape and touch the cow has won. This game is called Sambwen.

---

[39] *Kigelia africana.*

The old men likewise have their game. This is played on a board containing many compartments, in which they circulate pebbles called 'n-doto. This game is called en-geshei.

The warriors also play this game, but they do not care about it much. They have no boards, and make holes in the earth.

Peace Ceremonies

If the Masai make peace with other people, whether enemies or other Masai with whom they have fought, the warriors seize two important elders, and take a cow which has a calf, and a woman who has a baby; and the enemy do the same.

They then meet together at a certain spot, everybody present holding grass in his right hand, and exchange the cattle, the Masai taking the enemy's cow and the enemy the Masais'. The enemy's child is suckled at the breast of the Masai woman, and the Masai baby at the breast of the woman belonging to the enemy.

After this they return to their kraals, knowing that a solemn peace has been entered into.

Thus was peace restored between the Lumbwa Masai and the Masai proper, in the year of the sun,[40] at the place called the Ford of Sangaruna.[41]

Formerly when the Masai did not wish to make a solemn peace with the savages, they entered into blood brotherhood with them.

A Masai elder would sit down with one of the elders of the savages; each of them would then cut his left arm, and after dipping in the blood some meat of a bullock which was killed on the spot, would eat it.

When they had finished, the Masai went away, but they did not keep the peace.

[40] The year of the great famine (1883).
[41] On the Ruvu or Pangani River.

The Ceremony of the Red Bead

When a Masai wishes to make a person his brother or sister, he gives that person a red bead, called ol-tureshi. After performing this ceremony, they call one another Patureshi, i.e. The giver and receiver of a bead, instead of by their proper names.

Omens

The Masai believe in what they term Il-tiloi, or omens.

If a man goes to visit a woman who is ill, and the bird which is called Ol-tilo,[42] on account of its note, cries on his left hand, he knows that the woman is very ill indeed. Should the bird utter its cry on his right hand, he knows that the woman is on a fair way to recovery.

If a person visits a man who is unwell, and hears the same bird crying on his left hand, he knows that the man is only indisposed; but on the other hand, if a bird cries out on the right side of the road, he knows that the man will die.

Again, if a man goes to fight or to raid and hears the Tilo bird crying on his right hand, he knows that he will be successful. Should the sound come from the left hand, he will return home again, as he knows he will be beaten.

If a man is going to pay a visit and hears a Tilo bird behind him, it is a good omen, and he may expect to be received hospitably.

Should a person be traveling and hear several of these birds behind him, he must hasten, as it is a sign of rain.

If a man is going anywhere and meets another man walking alone, it is a bad sign: he continues on his way, but he knows that his journey will be in vain.

---

[42] *Mesopicus spodocephalus.*

The Medicine Men

Medicine men have four methods of divining future events.

The first is by means of a buffalo or ox horn. A handful of stones[43] is thrown in, and they know what is going to happen by the number which fall out when the horn is shaken.

The second is by examining the entrails of a goat which they slaughter. From what they see there they are able to predict that certain things will come to pass, such as epidemics, etc.

The third method is when they drink honey wine and get drunk. They are then able to prophesy what will take place.

The fourth method is by dreams. They tell people what they saw in their dreams, and it is believed to be a prophecy. Should the dream not come true after an interval of some years, people cannot say it is not correct: they must wait until the medicine man tells them that the event is about to happen.

If the medicine man is going to prophesy by means of the buffalo or ox horn, and there are people on the road, he tells those present that he will wait, as their feet will spoil his prophecy. They always know when people are coming, even if they are far off.

When a medicine man makes medicine, he gets drunk before he prophesies. He sings in parables, and the people reply.

For instance, when the medicine man named The Father of Ngupe made medicine for the warriors of Kilepo before they went on a raiding expedition, he sang:

> "The bulls that cannot move because they are so fat,
>   They will be beaten by Kilepo.
>   The bulls that cannot move because they are so fat,
>   Half of them have been captured."

The warriors of Kilepo went on their projected raid against the people of Kahe,[44] and captured half of their cattle.

They said: "Thus prophesied the medicine man."

---

[43] See note 49 on page 94 below.

All medicine men belong to the Kidongi family of the Aiser clan, and they are the descendants of Ol-Oimooja or of E-Sigiriaishi,[45] the sons of Ol-le-Mweiya.[46]

Of all the medicine men Lenana is the greatest. All Masai acknowledge him as their lord and pay tribute to him.

It is said that Lenana is the son of Mbatian, who was the son of Supeet, who was the son of Sitonik, who was the son of Kipepete, who was the son of Parinyombe, who was the son of Kidongoi, who was the son of E-Sigiriaishi, the son of Ol-le-Mweiya.

The story of the origin of the medicine men is said to be as follows: Ol-le-Mweiya came down from heaven and was found by the Aiser clan sitting on the top of their mountain.[47] He was such a small person that he was first of all believed to be a child. He was taken by the Aiser clan to their kraal, where it was discovered that he was a medicine man. He married and had issue.

When he was dying he said to his children: "Do not move from this spot." On account of this the Aiser clan do not go far from their mountain.

Now, of all the medicine men who lived in olden days Mbatian was the greatest.

It is said that formerly, before Europeans ever came to these countries, he prophesied that white people would arrive.

Again, before he died he told the people to move their grazing grounds, "for," he said, "all the cattle will die. You will first of all see flies which make hives like bees, then the wild beasts will die, and afterwards the cattle."

Both of these prophesies have come true: the Europeans have arrived, and the cattle died.

---

[44] A small state near Kilima Njaro.
[45] The Somali.
[46] The son of sickness (?).
[47] Commonly known to Europeans as Ngong or Donyo Lamuyu. The Masai have three names for this mountain—Eng-oñgu e-'m-bagasi (the eye *or* source of the Athi River), Ol-doinyo loo-'l-Aiser, and Ol-doinyo lo-'l-le-Mweiya.

Mbatian himself died while the cattle plague was raging (circa 1890).

When on the point of death, he called the elders of Matapato, the subdistrict in which he lived, and said to them: "Do not move from your country for I am about to die, and I will send you cattle from heaven. If you move, you will die of smallpox, your cattle will all perish, you will have to fight with a powerful enemy, and you will be beaten. I wish my successor to be the son to whom I give the medicine man's insignia. Obey him."

The elders said: "Very well," and left.

When they had gone, Mbatian called his eldest son Sendeyo,[48] and said to him: "Come tomorrow morning for I wish to give you the medicine man's insignia."

Sendeyo replied: "Very well," and went to lie down.

While this was taking place, Lenana, who had hidden himself in the calf shed, overheard the conversation. He arose early in the morning and went to his father's hut. On his arrival he said: "Father I have come."

Now Mbatian was very aged and he had only one eye. He therefore did not see which of his sons was before him and gave to Lenana the insignia of the medicine man (the iron club and the medicine horn, the gourd, the stones,[49] and the bag), at the same time saying: "Thou shalt be great among thy brothers and among all the people."

Lenana took the medicine man's insignia and went away.

Sendeyo then went to his father, but was told that his brother had already been there and been given the medicine man's insignia. When he heard this, he was very angry and said: "I will not be subject to my brother; I will fight with him till I kill him."

Mbatian died and was buried near Donyo Erok.

When he was dead, some of the people proclaimed Lenana principal medicine man, "for," they said, "Mbatian told us that he would give the insignia of his office to whichever of his sons

---

[48] Lenana is sometimes said to be the eldest son of Mbatian.

[49] According to tradition, these stones were brought many years ago from the north. It is asserted that no European has ever been allowed to behold them.

he wished should succeed him." They therefore remained with Lenana.

But others said: "We will not acknowledge this man for he is a cheat," and they threw in their lot with Sendeyo.[50]

Now disease broke out among Sendeyo's people, many of whom died, their cattle all perished, and they were defeated by the Germans; while those people who remained with Lenana did not fall ill, and they obtained cattle, as Mbatian had predicted.

The two rivals waged war for many years, and eventually Sendeyo was beaten. He came in 1902 to beg his brother to allow him to live with him, and peace was concluded between the two parties.

Before Lenana dies he will select whichever of his sons is acquainted with the work of the medicine men to succeed him.

The principal badge of the medicine man's office is the iron club.[51] If the medicine man sends a messenger to tell his people anything, he also sends his club so that it may be known that the message comes from him.

Should a medicine man strike anybody with the iron club, that person sickens and dies. It is said that Mbatian often struck people with his club, and waited until they were about to die, when he gave them medicine and cured them. Lenana, however, is a gentle man and does not kill people in this manner.

---

[50] This is the story as told by the Masai. The official version is that Lenana was chosen by the elders of most of the clans and districts on his father's death, but that Sendeyo refused to acknowledge him, and was supported by the 'L-oitai (i.e. the Masai of the 'L-oita subdistrict, near Kilima Njaro), with whom he lived for many years. The warriors of the two parties frequently met in deadly strife, and raided each other's cattle. In 1902 Sendeyo gave up the hopeless conflict, and agreed to acknowledge his brother as chief. He now lives not far from Naivasha. Lenana himself says that he and his three brothers Sendeyo, Neliang, and Tolito were examined by their father a short time before the latter's death, and as he possessed a better knowledge of the work of the medicine men than his brothers, he was given the iron club, etc., and chosen by the elders as Mbatian's successor.

[51] On one occasion the iron club was lost. A messenger was sent by Lenana to the Government authorities at Nairobi, and when crossing the Uganda Railway he was overtaken by a train. He jumped on one side and saved his life, but dropped the club, which was never found again. Its place was taken for some years by a small iron poker, but another club has now been made.

The Smiths[52]

All Masai do not know how to make spears and swords; this is the work of the smiths. It is they who make the weapons, and the others purchase from them.

The smiths use in the forge a stone, a hammer, pincers, and bellows, and they make needles, bracelets, axes, anklets, weapons, and other things.

The iron which they work with they purchase from the Swahili, or they smelt the ore which they find in the bed of the Matapato river.

Every clan has its smiths; but there is one clan, the Kipuyoni, to which most men of this class belong.

The other Masai do not marry the daughters of the smiths, for it is not considered correct. The smiths marry among themselves.

If a Masai takes in his hand a spear or sword or other thing which a smith has held, he first of all oils his hand for it is considered improper for him to take it in his bare hand.

The smiths are not rich in cattle like other Masai. They have no luck with cattle. If you find one possessing forty head, it is a very large number.

The smiths have their own language, which, although a corruption of Masai, is not understood by the ordinary Masai. Not all of them can speak this language: it is only a certain number of them who know it.

---

[52] The Kunono and Dorobo seem to hold much the same position among the Masai as the Tumalods (smiths) and Ramis (hunters) among the Somali. No free Somali enters a smith, or shakes hands with a smith; none takes a wife from this stock, or gives his daughter to a member of it. The Tumalods are spread over the whole of Somaliland as the Kunono over Masailand, and no instance is known of them giving up the trade. Still more debased and poorer are the Ramis, who, like the Dorobo, live by hunting game.

Earthenware Pots and Gourds

Some Masai women are able to make earthenware pots; others who are unable to make them buy them from savages.

Gourds are also bought, or they are collected in the deserted kraals.

One pot can be purchased for a goat.

When the Masai make pots they make them in two sizes, big and small; these pots are also provided with handles by which they can be picked up.

When warriors go to the woods to slaughter cattle, they carry their cooking-pots by a strip of hide fastened to the handles.

Pipes

Old men among the Masai make pipes of goats' bones, rhinoceros horns, or pieces of wood. They do not, however, smoke much; they prefer to take snuff or chew tobacco.

The Divisions of the Day

The Masai have various names for the divisions of day and night.

There is day (as compared to night) and evening.

The evening is the time when the cattle return to the kraals just before the sun sets (6 P.M.).

There is also the time called Nightfall, or the hour for gossip (8 P.M.); this is the hour before people go to bed.

Then there is the night, midnight, and the time when the buffaloes go to drink—this latter is the hour before the sun rises, which the Swahili call *Saa kumi* (4 A.M.).

There is also the time called The blood-red period *or* When the sun decorates the sky: this is the hour when the first rays of the sun redden the heavens (6 A.M.).

Then there is the morning; this is after the sun has risen.

There are also the hours called The sun stands *or* is opposite to one (midday), The shadows lower themselves (1–2 P.M.), and Afternoon.

Seasons and Months

There are four seasons and twelve months.

The months of showers:

1. June. This is the month after the rain of the Pleiades, and the first month of the year.

2. July. The women wrangle and squabble because the cows give but little milk.

3. August. The grass having become dry, food for the cattle is only found in the valleys.

The months of hunger:

1. September. The trees flower in this month.

2. October. This is the last month of hunger. When it is finished the lesser rains may be expected.

3. November. The clouds become white.

The months of the lesser rains:

1. December. This is the month when the lesser rains fall in showers and the ground looks like stools or cloths for carrying children in.

2. January. The sun comes out again, and the lesser rains stop.

3. February. This is the last month of the lesser rains, when flocks of small birds *(Buphaga?)* follow the cattle.

The months of plenty:

1. March. This is the month when the rains of the Pleiades commence. The clouds become black, and heavy mists hang about.

2. April. The bulls have to be tied up in the kraals to prevent their being lost.

3. May. The Pleiades set in this month.

Should the rains still continue at the beginning of June, the

Masai say: "We have forgotten, this is May"; and should the hot season not be over at the commencement of December, they say: "We have forgotten, this is November."[53]

Yawning, Hiccoughs, Sneezing, and Illnesses

When the Masai yawn, they are said to be sleepy. If a small child yawns, his mother grasps his mouth between her fingers to prevent it from stretching and becoming big like the savages' mouths.

If a person has hiccoughs, it is believed that he will eat some meat.

When a person sneezes, he says to himself: "Somebody is calling me." If other people are present, they say to him: "May God make your head hard," or: "Have good health."

When a Masai falls ill, it is said to be God's sickness. Some people know of medicines, which they give to sick people to cure them.

Trees and Medicines

There are many trees (medicines) of which the Masai make use.

The following medicines are used as purgatives:

1. *Embelia kilimandscharica,* Gilg. A concoction made from the bark of this so-called red tree mixed with butter. Also the berries of this tree, called The bitter things, which are chewed, or crushed and mixed with hot milk or blood.

2. The bark of *Croton elliottianus,* Engl. and Pax, mixed with curdled milk.

3. *Albizzia anthelminthica,* A. Brongn. The bark is mixed with

---

[53] The thirteen lunar months of the solar year are doubtless thus accounted for.

milk or blood or soup as a remedy for worms. This medicine is also good for nervous complaints.

4. *Euphorbia polyacantha,* Boiss. This plant, which has the same medicinal qualities as *Albizzia anthelminthica,* is cut up into small pieces and drunk in hot milk or water.

5. *Commiphora sp.* The bark of this tree is boiled in milk and drunk hot.

6. *Euphorbia sp.* Children eat this if they are unwell, for it does them no harm.

The following medicines are used as fever medicines:

1. *Cassia (?).* The crushed bark mixed with milk or blood and water is drunk by a fever-stricken person. It is very hot, and when chewed tastes like pepper.

2. The roots and fruit of *Solanum campylacanthum,* Hochst., are mixed with hot milk and drunk.

3. *Acacia albida,* Delile. The bark is stripped off and boiled. The patient drinks this and vomits, after which he recovers.

4. Blood and hot milk are drunk.

5. *Zanthoxylum sp.* Babies are given a piece of the bark to chew as a preventive against fever, for the Masai say: "The fever is afraid of this tree."

The medicines used to cause vomiting:

1. *Lippia sp.* soaked in boiling water.

2. A goat is slaughtered and the undigested food from the intestines is taken by the patient.

3. *Harrisonia abyssinica,* Oliver. The roots are put into hot water which is given to the patient.

4. Serum of a cow.[54]

5. *Terminalia sp.* Sick people are given the leaves to chew.

The medicine for nerve complaints:

Bauhinia reticulata, DC. The bark or roots are mixed with hot milk and drunk. Old men are very fond of this medicine.

Medicine for the spleen:

1. *Maba (?).* The roots are boiled, and the medicine is mixed with hot milk, which is drunk.

---

[54] See "Wounds and Surgeons," page 105 below.

2. *Euclea fructuosa,* Hiern. The boiled roots are mixed with honey.

3. *Loranthus sp.* The roots are mixed with soup.

The medicines used by the warriors in their slaughterhouses:

1. *Acacia abyssinica,* Hochst. When Masai warriors slaughter a bullock, they make a medicine out of the bark and roots of this tree. This they mix with soup and drink out of the stomach of the bullock. Warriors who have been wounded are also given this medicine in water to quench the thirst.

2. *Pappea capensis, forma foliis maioribus,* Radlk. Warriors like drinking water in which some of the crushed bark of this tree has been soaked. The water becomes blood-red in appearance and the warriors gain in courage.

3. *Acacia sp.* Warriors also become brave when they drink a medicine made out of the bark of this tree.

4, 5. *Grewia villosa,* Willd., and *Croton zambesicus,* Müll. Arg. A strengthening medicine is obtained from the roots of these trees, which is mixed with mutton soup.

The trees from which rope is made:

1. *Adansonia digitata,* L.

2. *Kigelia africana,* Bth.[55]

3. *Sanseviera cylindrica,* Boj.

4. *Acacia seyal,* Delile.

5. *Acacia merkeri,* Harms.

6. *Acacia robusta,* Burch.

7. *Musa ensete,* J. F. Gmel.

The tree from which the warriors obtain the cord for binding their plaits with:

Ficus, near *F. elegans,* Miq.

If one man curses another, and the curse takes effect, the man who has been cursed calls the other and asks him to spit on him and to tie on his arm a strip of cord made from this fig tree. The cord is first of all dipped in hot milk and then four beads are threaded on it.

The trees used by the medicine men in making their medicines:

---

[55] Or *Kigelia pinnata,* DC.

1. The heartwood of *Juniperus procera,* Hochst.

2. The roots and stalks of *Lantana sp.*

3. *Cordia ovalis,* R. Br. This tree is thought much of by the Masai, and a charm made from it, which the medicine men use, is called Ol-okora.

It has, too, an edible fruit, called The berries of the Cordia, which the children are fond of.

4. The bark of *Courbonia virgata,* Brongn.

5. The roots of *Osyris tenuifolia,* Engl.

The trees which are used for fumigating the milk gourds:

The women clean the milk gourds with cows' urine and a twig of the doum palm (*Hyphaene thebaica,* Mart.), the end of which has been chewed till it resembles a brush.

The gourd is then fumigated by means of a smoldering piece of wood, after which it is dusted out with a cow's tail kept especially for this purpose.

The trees which are used for fumigating are:

1. *Olea chrysophylla,* Lam.

2. *Cordia rothii,* Roem. and Schult.

3. *Zanthoxylum sp.*

4. *Premna oligotricha,* Baker.

5. *Grewia sp.*

The trees which the warriors and girls use for scent:

1. The flowers of *Justicia fischeri,* Lindau.

2. The roots of *Lantana sp.*

3. The leaves of *Tarchonanthus camphoratus,* Houtt., which they wear in their ears.

4. The leaves of *Urticaceous sp.,* which grows at the water's edge.

5. *Indigofera sp.* This is plaited and hung round the neck.

6. The flowers and leaves of *Ocimum suave,* Willd.

7. People like to lie on the leaves of *Clausena inaequalis,* Benth., as they are sweet-scented. The warriors also carry some in their hands when they go to the dances; and the branches of this plant are used as toothbrushes.

8. The roots of *Dregea rubicunda,* K. Sch., which are worn in the hair.

The tree used for binding shields:

Acacia pennata, Willd., the spine of which is used to sew the edge of the shields with.

The warriors also make their meat skewers of this tree.

The trees from which the clubs and the spear handles are made:

1. *Olea chrysophylla,* Lam.
2. *Albizzia sp.*
3. *Teclea unifoliolata,* Baill.
4. *Cordia rothii,* Roem. and Schult.
5. *Ochna merkeri,* Gilg.

Other trees which are made use of:

1. *Grewia bicolor,* Juss., and *Tamarindus indica,* L. From these trees sticks are cut.

2. The warriors use bamboo for the framework of their ostrich feather headdresses, which they wear when they go to the wars.

The old men also use bamboo for their tobacco pouches.

3. *Acokanthera schimperi* (Hochst.), Bth. and Hook. The Dorobo obtain poison for their arrows from this tree, and Masai elders purchase it from them.

4. *Balanites sp.* With the thorns of this tree the Masai pierce their children's ears. The sap, called gum or frankincense, is chewed by women, and is used for mending the gourds when they break.

5. *Rubica cordifolia,* L., and *Plumbago zeylanica,* L. There are two plants called ol-ngeriandus, from one of which a dye is obtained which is used for coloring the sheaths red, while the other is used for tattooing.

The latter kind is what girls like, and they tattoo themselves with it on the forehead and the sides of the face to make themselves look beautiful; but it is only done by those who wish, it is not done by force.

Girls also scratch the skin off their bellies with thorns, or make incisions with grass round their navels, but they do not rub anything into these cuts.

Some warriors do this too, but only those who wish.

6. *Terminalia sp.* The tannin of this tree is used by the women for curing skins with. It is also given to cattle when they are suffering from gall fever.

7. *Lantana salvifolia,* Jacq. The leaves and fruit of this plant are used by the Masai to mix with oil, with which they anoint their bodies.

8. *Mœrua uniflora,* Vahl. The warriors burn this plant and obtain a black dye from the ashes, with which they color their shields.

9. Women and girls place the leaves of *Ricinus communis,* L., under their iron armlets and anklets to prevent them from chafing the skin.

10. *Commiphora sp.* Honey barrels are made of the wood of this tree.

How Fire Is Obtained

When the Masai move and go far,[56] the men take with them, or cut on the spot where they intend to stay, a hard pointed stick and a flat piece of wood. They then search for some donkey's dung or dry grass, and produce fire in the center of the new kraal by drilling the stick into a hole in the wood. When the fire has reached the grass they set light to some leaves of *Cordia ovalis* and throw wood onto the fire. The women obtain their fire from the one which the men have made.

The Masai say that the hard stick is a man and the flat piece of wood his wife.

The hard sticks are cut from *Ficus sycomorus* and *Ekebergia sp.;* the flat pieces of wood from any fibrous tree, such as *Kigelia africana, Cordia ovalis,* or *Acacia albida.*

Wounds and Surgeons

If a Masai warrior is shot, and an arm or leg broken, the surgeons are able to mend it.

---

[56] When the journey is a short one the women carry fire with them.

They cut through the flesh, take out the splinters and bring the edges of the bone together, after which they stitch up the wound with the sinew from the back of an ox, and bind the limb securely.

The only food that is given to a man with a broken limb is roast meat and the thirst-quenching medicine obtained from *Acacia abyssinica.*.

Should a man be shot in the belly so that the intestines protrude, the wound is washed and the intestines returned to their place; sheep's fat (a quart or more) is poured into the wound, which is then stitched up.

Again, if a man is shot and a rib broken, the flesh is skinned from the wound, and a sheep's rib is inserted in place of the broken one. Sheep's fat is then poured into the wound, after which it is sewn up.

The wounded man is not allowed to drink milk, and may only eat meat.

If a man is shot with a poisoned arrow, a pregnant cow is slaughtered, and he is given the caul fat to drink. This causes him to vomit and he recovers.

If the surgeons see that a man's bone cannot be mended, they fasten a ligature round the limb and amputate it.

The surgeons are also able to castrate bulls, rams, and he-goats by either removing or crushing the testicles. When bulls are castrated, a cord is fastened tightly round their necks and blood is extracted from the jugular veins to prevent inflammation of the injured parts.

Masai Curses

May you be clothed with an incurable disease!
    May God trouble you!
    May a beast of prey devour you!
    Slip on the road and fall!
    May you become the color of a corpse!

May God give you a palm of leather! (i.e. may your cattle die, in which case you will be forced to do manual labor.)

Die with those who have been conquered!

Die when the sun sets!

Die in the plain!

May your own people kill you!

When the Masai curse children, they do not call them very bad names. They say, for instance:

Stone!

Pit!

Masai Form of Oath

If a Masai man says something, and it is believed to be a lie, it is true if he adds: "By my sister's garment."

Likewise if a Masai woman adds: "By my father's garment," it is true.

Trial by Ordeal Among the Masai

Some Masai have a trial by ordeal.

If a person is accused of having done something wrong, he drinks some blood, which is given him by the spokesman, and says: "If I have done this deed, may God kill me."

If he has committed the crime, he dies; but if not, no harm befalls him.

Songs and Prayers

A Prayer to God[57]

Masai women do as follows when one of their number gives birth to a child.

They collect together and take milk to the mother; they then slaughter a sheep, which is called, The purifier of the hut, or simply The purifier.

The women slaughter the animal by themselves, and eat all the meat.

No man may approach the spot where the animal is slaughtered, for it is considered unlawful.

When the women have finished their meal, they stand up and sing the following song:

Solo. The God! the God! whom I pray, my,
  Give me the offspring.
  Who thunders and it rains,
Chorus. Thee every day only I pray to thee.
Solo. Morning star which rises hither,
Chorus. Thee every day only I pray to thee.
Solo. He to whom I offer prayer is like sage,
Chorus. Thee every day only I pray to thee.
Solo. Who is prayed to, and He hears,
Chorus. Thee every day only I pray to thee.

They then sing another song as follows:

Solo. O girls, (friends) of the well-dressed one.
Chorus. Let us dress well, O my mother.
Solo. Ho! The day
  On which thy child is born, O my joy!
Chorus. Ho! He! Hoo! Ya! Ye! Hoo!

---

[57] Masai women often pray twice daily. Men and children usually only pray in time of drought, or when a cattle plague is raging.

A. C. Hollis

The Women's Prayer for Rain

If there is a drought, the women collect together, and, having tied grass onto their clothes, they sing as follows:

Solo. Our herbs of the Earth's back.
Chorus. Hie! Wae! Almighty.
Solo. The father of my Nasira[58] has conquered, has conquered,
Chorus. The highlands and also the lowlands
   Of our vast country which belongs to our God.
Solo. May this be our year, ours,
Chorus. O messenger of Mbatian's son.

The Old Men's Prayer in Time of Drought

If there is no rain, the old men light a bonfire of cordia wood, into which is thrown the medicine man's charm called ol-okora. They then encircle the fire and sing as follows:

Solo. The black god! ho!
Chorus. God, water us!
   O the of the uttermost parts of the earth![59]
Solo. The black god! ho!
Chorus. God, water us!

The Children's Song for Rain

When there is no rain the children sing as follows:

Solo. Rain, fall!
Chorus. That the hide does not choke me,

---

[58] Nasira was Mbatian's daughter, and half-sister to Lenana.
[59] Lit. The of the horn.

The old skin
Which takes away the ashes.

Songs in Time of War

Whenever Masai warriors wish to go to the wars, they first of all visit the medicine man, and as soon as he has given them medicine, they start.

When the old men are bidding their warrior sons farewell, they pour both milk and honey wine on to the ground, "for," they say, "God wishes it." The women sprinkle the warriors from a milk gourd.

On their arrival at the enemy's country, should the enemy offer fight, the warriors plant their swords in the earth and stand by them, saying at the same time: "I am the son of so-and-so; whether I die or conquer, it will be in this place."

If the enemy flees, the warriors pursue and slaughter them, and when they have killed them, they sing the following song while driving off the cattle:

Solo. I pray (that this may be)
  my year, whom I pray to is God.
Chorus. Wo-ho! Woo-hoo!
  Wo-ho! Woo-hoo!
Solo. I pray (that this may be)
  my year, whom I pray to is Lenana.
Chorus. Wo-ho! Woo-hoo!
  Wo-ho! Woo-hoo!
Solo. Our medicine man, Our medicine man,
  We tell thee the kraals in which are the bullocks.
Chorus. Wo-ho! Woo-hoo!
  Wo-ho! Woo-hoo!

When warriors tarry on a raid, their mothers, sisters, and lovers collect outside the huts on the appearance of the morning star in the heavens, and pray to God.

They tie grass onto their clothes, and leave milk in their

gourds, for they say: "Our children will soon be returning, and when they arrive they may be hungry."

When they have all collected together, they sing as follows:

Solo. The God to whom I pray, and he hears.
Chorus. The God to whom I pray for offspring.
Solo. I pray the heavenly bodies which have risen.
Chorus. The God to whom I pray for offspring.
Solo. Return hither our children
Chorus. Return hither our children.

There is another prayer to God, which is sung when the warriors tarry on a raid. All the women collect together, and, while holding in their hands small gourds covered with green grass, sing as follows:

I
Solo. God! God! tear out
Chorus. The brand marks of the people!
Solo. Tear out, tear out
Chorus. The brand marks of the people![60]
II
Solo. Girls, be not silent.
Chorus. It is being prayed to God.
Solo. Tear out, tear out
Chorus. The brand marks of the people!
III
Solo. Venus who is rising
Chorus. And the evening star.
Solo. Tear out
Chorus. The brand marks of the people!

IV
Solo. The clouds of snow-capped mountains, tear out
Chorus. The brand marks of the people!
Solo. (He) Who waits till the heavens are red,[61] tear out
Chorus. The brand marks of the people!

---

[60] The meaning here is Break the power of the foe.
[61] The sun.

When warriors return from the wars, they sing the following song on approaching their kraals:

Solo. The milkmen go behind us.
   We have conquered with the headdresses of the lion's mane.
Chorus. Yoa! I burn! Yoa! I burn!
   Yoa! I burn! Yoa! I burn!

Warriors' Songs

When Masai warriors kill barbarians in a fight, they paint the right half of their bodies red and the left half white.
   The comrades of those who have killed some of the enemy then sing their praises.
   The following is an example of their songs:

Solo. The pigtail on the top of your head
   Is about to be seized
   When you remember the kraals,
Chorus. O warrior son of Ol-Poruo.

   The following are other examples:

Solo. Ol-le-Langoi, the warrior who has reddened the ground with the blood
   Of those whose country had not been reconnoitered.
Chorus. Who ran on ahead and returned in the evening to the van.
Solo. I tell you he has killed. *(Chorus)* How often? *(Solo)* Three times in one month.
Chorus. The cows with the crumpled horns which were shown to Ainsworth[62] were in the kraal.
   We captured them because he climbed to Kimara[63] to take the place of those who had retired.

---

[62] J. Ainsworth, sub-commissioner, Ukamba Province.
[63] Kimara is the Masai name for a district in Kikuyu.

Solo. It came to pass that we heard the lowing of the kine,
Chorus. He ran (until he captured them), our Medoto of the splendid shield.

Solo. The people of Marangu and Moishi[64] are in terror.
Chorus. Place the son of Parmet in the van of the fight.
Solo. When you did not kill anybody,
Chorus. We did not leave our hut, blood-red is our sign.

Solo. It is said the son of Tema has an ostrich feather headdress which has not been worn.
Chorus. I did not refuse to give you the credit of killing the herdsman.
Solo. They are seeking a stronger herdsman for you now.
Chorus. You killed another by the doum palm as we entered the country.

EN-GIDIPATA

---

[64] Marangu and Moshi are two of the Chaga States on Kilima Njaro.

Index

Adultery, 83
Ages and generations: *see* Masai.
Antelope, 30, 89.
Anthill with two exits, 25.

Barbarian, savage (Bantu), 8, 73, 83, 88, 90, 97; origin of, 54.
Barren women, 19, 61, 81.
Beads, 10, 47, 62, 88, 91, 102.
Birds, 71, 73, 88, 89, 91, 98.
Birth, 79, 107.
Blood as food, 87, 100, 106.
Blood money, 83.
Brand marks, 67, 110.
Buffalo, 32, 88.
Burial: *see* Dead.
Butterfly, 47.

Cannibalism, 9, 19.
Castration, 105.
Caterpillar, 21.
Cattle, 4, 6, 15, 20, 22, 25, 50, 66, 76, 81, 87, 109, 111; and ghosts, 81; branding and cutting ears, 67; descending from heaven, 51, 53, 94; disease foretold by medicine man, 94; hide, 6, 12, 45, 52, 53, 71; method of slaughtering, 75; names, 23, 24, 66; skull placed near door of hut, 70.
Caul fat, 41, 59, 105.
Caves, myths regarding, 61.
Chaga tribe, 112.
Chief, 31: *see also* Warriors.
Children, adrift, 19; out of knee, 12.
Circumcision, adult, 2, 4, 8, 20, 70, 71, 74.

Clans and families: *see* Masai.
Clouds, prayer to, 110.
Comet, myths regarding, 58.
Cooking pots, 97.
Counselor, 26, 72, 75; club of, 89.
Cowardice, 3, 8, 73.
Crimes, 82; punishment of, 19, 25, 82.
Crow, 26.
Cupping, 2, 47, 87.
Curse, 78, 83, 102, 105.

Day, myth regarding, 59; divisions of, 97.
Dead, disposal of, 41, 54, 78, 79, 95.
Death, 78.
Demon or devil, 3, 6, 30; animals out of toe of, 4; animals and men out of fingers of, 31; change of appearance, 50; man out of face of, 31.
Districts and subdistricts: *see* Masai.
Divorce, 77.
Dolls, 89.
Donkeys, braying at moon, 56; ear cutting, 67; herding, 20; saddling, 69.
Dorobo, hunting tribe, 32, 33, 50, 53, 67, 73, 87, 96.
Dress, boys wearing women's, 73; of old men, 46, 58, 74, 106; of warriors, 62, 63, 71, 76; of women and girls, 40, 42, 47, 62, 63, 77, 103, 106, 108; warriors exchanging, 83.

Ear cutting, 67, 79.
Earth, 40; and sky, myth regarding, 60.

War, 4, 8, 20, 23, 27, 29, 92, 109; reason
for waging, against other tribes,
52; songs, 108 ff.
Warriors, praising the brave, 67, 111;
selection of a chief, 74; titles, 73.
Weapons, Dorobo, 34; of boys, 72,
73; of old men, 14, 47, 68; of warriors, 2, 11, 23, 68, 71.

Wild animals, 88–89.
Wildebeest, 89.
Wounds, treatment of, 105.

Yawning, 99.

Zebra, 36, 41.

A CATALOG OF SELECTED
DOVER BOOKS
IN ALL FIELDS OF INTEREST

A CATALOG OF SELECTED DOVER
BOOKS IN ALL FIELDS OF INTEREST

CONCERNING THE SPIRITUAL IN ART, Wassily Kandinsky. Pioneering work by father of abstract art. Thoughts on color theory, nature of art. Analysis of earlier masters. 12 illustrations. 80pp. of text. 5⅜ x 8½.   23411-8

ANIMALS: 1,419 Copyright-Free Illustrations of Mammals, Birds, Fish, Insects, etc., Jim Harter (ed.). Clear wood engravings present, in extremely lifelike poses, over 1,000 species of animals. One of the most extensive pictorial sourcebooks of its kind. Captions. Index. 284pp. 9 x 12.   23766-4

CELTIC ART: The Methods of Construction, George Bain. Simple geometric techniques for making Celtic interlacements, spirals, Kells-type initials, animals, humans, etc. Over 500 illustrations. 160pp. 9 x 12. (Available in U.S. only.)   22923-8

AN ATLAS OF ANATOMY FOR ARTISTS, Fritz Schider. Most thorough reference work on art anatomy in the world. Hundreds of illustrations, including selections from works by Vesalius, Leonardo, Goya, Ingres, Michelangelo, others. 593 illustrations. 192pp. 7⅛ x 10¼.   20241-0

CELTIC HAND STROKE-BY-STROKE (Irish Half-Uncial from "The Book of Kells"): An Arthur Baker Calligraphy Manual, Arthur Baker. Complete guide to creating each letter of the alphabet in distinctive Celtic manner. Covers hand position, strokes, pens, inks, paper, more. Illustrated. 48pp. 8¼ x 11.   24336-2

EASY ORIGAMI, John Montroll. Charming collection of 32 projects (hat, cup, pelican, piano, swan, many more) specially designed for the novice origami hobbyist. Clearly illustrated easy-to-follow instructions insure that even beginning papercrafters will achieve successful results. 48pp. 8¼ x 11.   27298-2

THE COMPLETE BOOK OF BIRDHOUSE CONSTRUCTION FOR WOODWORKERS, Scott D. Campbell. Detailed instructions, illustrations, tables. Also data on bird habitat and instinct patterns. Bibliography. 3 tables. 63 illustrations in 15 figures. 48pp. 5¼ x 8½.   24407-5

BLOOMINGDALE'S ILLUSTRATED 1886 CATALOG: Fashions, Dry Goods and Housewares, Bloomingdale Brothers. Famed merchants' extremely rare catalog depicting about 1,700 products: clothing, housewares, firearms, dry goods, jewelry, more. Invaluable for dating, identifying vintage items. Also, copyright-free graphics for artists, designers. Co-published with Henry Ford Museum & Greenfield Village. 160pp. 8¼ x 11.   25780-0

HISTORIC COSTUME IN PICTURES, Braun & Schneider. Over 1,450 costumed figures in clearly detailed engravings–from dawn of civilization to end of 19th century. Captions. Many folk costumes. 256pp. 8⅜ x 11¾.   23150-X

STICKLEY CRAFTSMAN FURNITURE CATALOGS, Gustav Stickley and L. & J. G. Stickley. Beautiful, functional furniture in two authentic catalogs from 1910. 594 illustrations, including 277 photos, show settles, rockers, armchairs, reclining chairs, bookcases, desks, tables. 183pp. 6½ x 9¼. 23838-5

AMERICAN LOCOMOTIVES IN HISTORIC PHOTOGRAPHS: 1858 to 1949, Ron Ziel (ed.). A rare collection of 126 meticulously detailed official photographs, called "builder portraits," of American locomotives that majestically chronicle the rise of steam locomotive power in America. Introduction. Detailed captions. xi+ 129pp. 9 x 12. 27393-8

AMERICA'S LIGHTHOUSES: An Illustrated History, Francis Ross Holland, Jr. Delightfully written, profusely illustrated fact-filled survey of over 200 American lighthouses since 1716. History, anecdotes, technological advances, more. 240pp. 8 x 10¾. 25576-X

TOWARDS A NEW ARCHITECTURE, Le Corbusier. Pioneering manifesto by founder of "International School." Technical and aesthetic theories, views of industry, economics, relation of form to function, "mass-production split" and much more. Profusely illustrated. 320pp. 6⅛ x 9¼. (Available in U.S. only.) 25023-7

HOW THE OTHER HALF LIVES, Jacob Riis. Famous journalistic record, exposing poverty and degradation of New York slums around 1900, by major social reformer. 100 striking and influential photographs. 233pp. 10 x 7⅞. 22012-5

FRUIT KEY AND TWIG KEY TO TREES AND SHRUBS, William M. Harlow. One of the handiest and most widely used identification aids. Fruit key covers 120 deciduous and evergreen species; twig key 160 deciduous species. Easily used. Over 300 photographs. 126pp. 5⅜ x 8½. 20511-8

COMMON BIRD SONGS, Dr. Donald J. Borror. Songs of 60 most common U.S. birds: robins, sparrows, cardinals, bluejays, finches, more—arranged in order of increasing complexity. Up to 9 variations of songs of each species.
Cassette and manual 99911-4

ORCHIDS AS HOUSE PLANTS, Rebecca Tyson Northen. Grow cattleyas and many other kinds of orchids—in a window, in a case, or under artificial light. 63 illustrations. 148pp. 5⅜ x 8½. 23261-1

MONSTER MAZES, Dave Phillips. Masterful mazes at four levels of difficulty. Avoid deadly perils and evil creatures to find magical treasures. Solutions for all 32 exciting illustrated puzzles. 48pp. 8¼ x 11. 26005-4

MOZART'S DON GIOVANNI (DOVER OPERA LIBRETTO SERIES), Wolfgang Amadeus Mozart. Introduced and translated by Ellen H. Bleiler. Standard Italian libretto, with complete English translation. Convenient and thoroughly portable—an ideal companion for reading along with a recording or the performance itself. Introduction. List of characters. Plot summary. 121pp. 5¼ x 8½. 24944-1

TECHNICAL MANUAL AND DICTIONARY OF CLASSICAL BALLET, Gail Grant. Defines, explains, comments on steps, movements, poses and concepts. 15-page pictorial section. Basic book for student, viewer. 127pp. 5⅜ x 8½. 21843-0

THE CLARINET AND CLARINET PLAYING, David Pino. Lively, comprehensive work features suggestions about technique, musicianship, and musical interpretation, as well as guidelines for teaching, making your own reeds, and preparing for public performance. Includes an intriguing look at clarinet history. "A godsend," *The Clarinet,* Journal of the International Clarinet Society. Appendixes. 7 illus. 320pp. 5⅜ x 8½. 40270-3

HOLLYWOOD GLAMOR PORTRAITS, John Kobal (ed.). 145 photos from 1926-49. Harlow, Gable, Bogart, Bacall; 94 stars in all. Full background on photographers, technical aspects. 160pp. 8⅜ x 11¼. 23352-9

THE ANNOTATED CASEY AT THE BAT: A Collection of Ballads about the Mighty Casey/Third, Revised Edition, Martin Gardner (ed.). Amusing sequels and parodies of one of America's best-loved poems: Casey's Revenge, Why Casey Whiffed, Casey's Sister at the Bat, others. 256pp. 5⅜ x 8½. 28598-7

THE RAVEN AND OTHER FAVORITE POEMS, Edgar Allan Poe. Over 40 of the author's most memorable poems: "The Bells," "Ulalume," "Israfel," "To Helen," "The Conqueror Worm," "Eldorado," "Annabel Lee," many more. Alphabetic lists of titles and first lines. 64pp. 5$\frac{3}{16}$ x 8¼. 26685-0

PERSONAL MEMOIRS OF U. S. GRANT, Ulysses Simpson Grant. Intelligent, deeply moving firsthand account of Civil War campaigns, considered by many the finest military memoirs ever written. Includes letters, historic photographs, maps and more. 528pp. 6⅛ x 9¼. 28587-1

ANCIENT EGYPTIAN MATERIALS AND INDUSTRIES, A. Lucas and J. Harris. Fascinating, comprehensive, thoroughly documented text describes this ancient civilization's vast resources and the processes that incorporated them in daily life, including the use of animal products, building materials, cosmetics, perfumes and incense, fibers, glazed ware, glass and its manufacture, materials used in the mummification process, and much more. 544pp. 6⅛ x 9¼. (Available in U.S. only.) 40446-3

RUSSIAN STORIES/RUSSKIE RASSKAZY: A Dual-Language Book, edited by Gleb Struve. Twelve tales by such masters as Chekhov, Tolstoy, Dostoevsky, Pushkin, others. Excellent word-for-word English translations on facing pages, plus teaching and study aids, Russian/English vocabulary, biographical/critical introductions, more. 416pp. 5⅜ x 8½. 26244-8

PHILADELPHIA THEN AND NOW: 60 Sites Photographed in the Past and Present, Kenneth Finkel and Susan Oyama. Rare photographs of City Hall, Logan Square, Independence Hall, Betsy Ross House, other landmarks juxtaposed with contemporary views. Captures changing face of historic city. Introduction. Captions. 128pp. 8¼ x 11. 25790-8

AIA ARCHITECTURAL GUIDE TO NASSAU AND SUFFOLK COUNTIES, LONG ISLAND, The American Institute of Architects, Long Island Chapter, and the Society for the Preservation of Long Island Antiquities. Comprehensive, well-researched and generously illustrated volume brings to life over three centuries of Long Island's great architectural heritage. More than 240 photographs with authoritative, extensively detailed captions. 176pp. 8¼ x 11. 26946-9

NORTH AMERICAN INDIAN LIFE: Customs and Traditions of 23 Tribes, Elsie Clews Parsons (ed.). 27 fictionalized essays by noted anthropologists examine religion, customs, government, additional facets of life among the Winnebago, Crow, Zuni, Eskimo, other tribes. 480pp. 6⅛ x 9¼. 27377-6

FRANK LLOYD WRIGHT'S DANA HOUSE, Donald Hoffmann. Pictorial essay of residential masterpiece with over 160 interior and exterior photos, plans, elevations, sketches and studies. 128pp. 9¹/₄ x 10¾. 29120-0

THE MALE AND FEMALE FIGURE IN MOTION: 60 Classic Photographic Sequences, Eadweard Muybridge. 60 true-action photographs of men and women walking, running, climbing, bending, turning, etc., reproduced from rare 19th-century masterpiece. vi + 121pp. 9 x 12. 24745-7

1001 QUESTIONS ANSWERED ABOUT THE SEASHORE, N. J. Berrill and Jacquelyn Berrill. Queries answered about dolphins, sea snails, sponges, starfish, fishes, shore birds, many others. Covers appearance, breeding, growth, feeding, much more. 305pp. 5¼ x 8¼. 23366-9

ATTRACTING BIRDS TO YOUR YARD, William J. Weber. Easy-to-follow guide offers advice on how to attract the greatest diversity of birds: birdhouses, feeders, water and waterers, much more. 96pp. 5³/₁₆ x 8¼. 28927-3

MEDICINAL AND OTHER USES OF NORTH AMERICAN PLANTS: A Historical Survey with Special Reference to the Eastern Indian Tribes, Charlotte Erichsen-Brown. Chronological historical citations document 500 years of usage of plants, trees, shrubs native to eastern Canada, northeastern U.S. Also complete identifying information. 343 illustrations. 544pp. 6½ x 9¼. 25951-X

STORYBOOK MAZES, Dave Phillips. 23 stories and mazes on two-page spreads: Wizard of Oz, Treasure Island, Robin Hood, etc. Solutions. 64pp. 8¼ x 11. 23628-5

AMERICAN NEGRO SONGS: 230 Folk Songs and Spirituals, Religious and Secular, John W. Work. This authoritative study traces the African influences of songs sung and played by black Americans at work, in church, and as entertainment. The author discusses the lyric significance of such songs as "Swing Low, Sweet Chariot," "John Henry," and others and offers the words and music for 230 songs. Bibliography. Index of Song Titles. 272pp. 6½ x 9¼. 40271-1

MOVIE-STAR PORTRAITS OF THE FORTIES, John Kobal (ed.). 163 glamor, studio photos of 106 stars of the 1940s: Rita Hayworth, Ava Gardner, Marlon Brando, Clark Gable, many more. 176pp. 8⅜ x 11¼. 23546-7

BENCHLEY LOST AND FOUND, Robert Benchley. Finest humor from early 30s, about pet peeves, child psychologists, post office and others. Mostly unavailable elsewhere. 73 illustrations by Peter Arno and others. 183pp. 5⅜ x 8½. 22410-4

YEKL and THE IMPORTED BRIDEGROOM AND OTHER STORIES OF YIDDISH NEW YORK, Abraham Cahan. Film Hester Street based on Yekl (1896). Novel, other stories among first about Jewish immigrants on N.Y.'s East Side. 240pp. 5⅜ x 8½. 22427-9

SELECTED POEMS, Walt Whitman. Generous sampling from Leaves of Grass. Twenty-four poems include "I Hear America Singing," "Song of the Open Road," "I Sing the Body Electric," "When Lilacs Last in the Dooryard Bloom'd," "O Captain! My Captain!"—all reprinted from an authoritative edition. Lists of titles and first lines. 128pp. 5³/₁₆ x 8¼. 26878-0

THE BEST TALES OF HOFFMANN, E. T. A. Hoffmann. 10 of Hoffmann's most important stories: "Nutcracker and the King of Mice," "The Golden Flowerpot," etc. 458pp. 5⅜ x 8½. 21793-0

FROM FETISH TO GOD IN ANCIENT EGYPT, E. A. Wallis Budge. Rich detailed survey of Egyptian conception of "God" and gods, magic, cult of animals, Osiris, more. Also, superb English translations of hymns and legends. 240 illustrations. 545pp. 5⅜ x 8½. 25803-3

FRENCH STORIES/CONTES FRANÇAIS: A Dual-Language Book, Wallace Fowlie. Ten stories by French masters, Voltaire to Camus: "Micromegas" by Voltaire; "The Atheist's Mass" by Balzac; "Minuet" by de Maupassant; "The Guest" by Camus, six more. Excellent English translations on facing pages. Also French-English vocabulary list, exercises, more. 352pp. 5⅜ x 8½. 26443-2

CHICAGO AT THE TURN OF THE CENTURY IN PHOTOGRAPHS: 122 Historic Views from the Collections of the Chicago Historical Society, Larry A. Viskochil. Rare large-format prints offer detailed views of City Hall, State Street, the Loop, Hull House, Union Station, many other landmarks, circa 1904-1913. Introduction. Captions. Maps. 144pp. 9⅜ x 12¼. 24656-6

OLD BROOKLYN IN EARLY PHOTOGRAPHS, 1865-1929, William Lee Younger. Luna Park, Gravesend race track, construction of Grand Army Plaza, moving of Hotel Brighton, etc. 157 previously unpublished photographs. 165pp. 8⅞ x 11¾. 23587-4

THE MYTHS OF THE NORTH AMERICAN INDIANS, Lewis Spence. Rich anthology of the myths and legends of the Algonquins, Iroquois, Pawnees and Sioux, prefaced by an extensive historical and ethnological commentary. 36 illustrations. 480pp. 5⅜ x 8½. 25967-6

AN ENCYCLOPEDIA OF BATTLES: Accounts of Over 1,560 Battles from 1479 B.C. to the Present, David Eggenberger. Essential details of every major battle in recorded history from the first battle of Megiddo in 1479 B.C. to Grenada in 1984. List of Battle Maps. New Appendix covering the years 1967-1984. Index. 99 illustrations. 544pp. 6½ x 9¼. 24913-1

SAILING ALONE AROUND THE WORLD, Captain Joshua Slocum. First man to sail around the world, alone, in small boat. One of great feats of seamanship told in delightful manner. 67 illustrations. 294pp. 5⅜ x 8½. 20326-3

ANARCHISM AND OTHER ESSAYS, Emma Goldman. Powerful, penetrating, prophetic essays on direct action, role of minorities, prison reform, puritan hypocrisy, violence, etc. 271pp. 5⅜ x 8½. 22484-8

MYTHS OF THE HINDUS AND BUDDHISTS, Ananda K. Coomaraswamy and Sister Nivedita. Great stories of the epics; deeds of Krishna, Shiva, taken from puranas, Vedas, folk tales; etc. 32 illustrations. 400pp. 5⅜ x 8½. 21759-0

THE TRAUMA OF BIRTH, Otto Rank. Rank's controversial thesis that anxiety neurosis is caused by profound psychological trauma which occurs at birth. 256pp. 5⅜ x 8½. 27974-X

A THEOLOGICO-POLITICAL TREATISE, Benedict Spinoza. Also contains unfinished Political Treatise. Great classic on religious liberty, theory of government on common consent. R. Elwes translation. Total of 421pp. 5⅜ x 8½. 20249-6

MY BONDAGE AND MY FREEDOM, Frederick Douglass. Born a slave, Douglass became outspoken force in antislavery movement. The best of Douglass' autobiographies. Graphic description of slave life. 464pp. 5⅜ x 8½. 22457-0

FOLLOWING THE EQUATOR: A Journey Around the World, Mark Twain. Fascinating humorous account of 1897 voyage to Hawaii, Australia, India, New Zealand, etc. Ironic, bemused reports on peoples, customs, climate, flora and fauna, politics, much more. 197 illustrations. 720pp. 5⅜ x 8½. 26113-1

THE PEOPLE CALLED SHAKERS, Edward D. Andrews. Definitive study of Shakers: origins, beliefs, practices, dances, social organization, furniture and crafts, etc. 33 illustrations. 351pp. 5⅜ x 8½. 21081-2

THE MYTHS OF GREECE AND ROME, H. A. Guerber. A classic of mythology, generously illustrated, long prized for its simple, graphic, accurate retelling of the principal myths of Greece and Rome, and for its commentary on their origins and significance. With 64 illustrations by Michelangelo, Raphael, Titian, Rubens, Canova, Bernini and others. 480pp. 5⅜ x 8½. 27584-1

PSYCHOLOGY OF MUSIC, Carl E. Seashore. Classic work discusses music as a medium from psychological viewpoint. Clear treatment of physical acoustics, auditory apparatus, sound perception, development of musical skills, nature of musical feeling, host of other topics. 88 figures. 408pp. 5⅜ x 8½. 21851-1

THE PHILOSOPHY OF HISTORY, Georg W. Hegel. Great classic of Western thought develops concept that history is not chance but rational process, the evolution of freedom. 457pp. 5⅜ x 8½. 20112-0

THE BOOK OF TEA, Kakuzo Okakura. Minor classic of the Orient: entertaining, charming explanation, interpretation of traditional Japanese culture in terms of tea ceremony. 94pp. 5⅜ x 8½. 20070-1

LIFE IN ANCIENT EGYPT, Adolf Erman. Fullest, most thorough, detailed older account with much not in more recent books, domestic life, religion, magic, medicine, commerce, much more. Many illustrations reproduce tomb paintings, carvings, hieroglyphs, etc. 597pp. 5⅜ x 8½. 22632-8

SUNDIALS, Their Theory and Construction, Albert Waugh. Far and away the best, most thorough coverage of ideas, mathematics concerned, types, construction, adjusting anywhere. Simple, nontechnical treatment allows even children to build several of these dials. Over 100 illustrations. 230pp. 5⅜ x 8½. 22947-5

THEORETICAL HYDRODYNAMICS, L. M. Milne-Thomson. Classic exposition of the mathematical theory of fluid motion, applicable to both hydrodynamics and aerodynamics. Over 600 exercises. 768pp. 6⅛ x 9¼. 68970-0

SONGS OF EXPERIENCE: Facsimile Reproduction with 26 Plates in Full Color, William Blake. 26 full-color plates from a rare 1826 edition. Includes "The Tyger," "London," "Holy Thursday," and other poems. Printed text of poems. 48pp. 5¼ x 7. 24636-1

OLD-TIME VIGNETTES IN FULL COLOR, Carol Belanger Grafton (ed.). Over 390 charming, often sentimental illustrations, selected from archives of Victorian graphics—pretty women posing, children playing, food, flowers, kittens and puppies, smiling cherubs, birds and butterflies, much more. All copyright-free. 48pp. 9¼ x 12¼. 27269-9

CATALOG OF DOVER BOOKS

PERSPECTIVE FOR ARTISTS, Rex Vicat Cole. Depth, perspective of sky and sea, shadows, much more, not usually covered. 391 diagrams, 81 reproductions of drawings and paintings. 279pp. 5⅜ x 8½.
22487-2

DRAWING THE LIVING FIGURE, Joseph Sheppard. Innovative approach to artistic anatomy focuses on specifics of surface anatomy, rather than muscles and bones. Over 170 drawings of live models in front, back and side views, and in widely varying poses. Accompanying diagrams. 177 illustrations. Introduction. Index. 144pp. 8⅜ x11¼.
26723-7

GOTHIC AND OLD ENGLISH ALPHABETS: 100 Complete Fonts, Dan X. Solo. Add power, elegance to posters, signs, other graphics with 100 stunning copyright-free alphabets: Blackstone, Dolbey, Germania, 97 more–including many lower-case, numerals, punctuation marks. 104pp. 8⅛ x 11.
24695-7

HOW TO DO BEADWORK, Mary White. Fundamental book on craft from simple projects to five-bead chains and woven works. 106 illustrations. 142pp. 5⅜ x 8.
20697-1

THE BOOK OF WOOD CARVING, Charles Marshall Sayers. Finest book for beginners discusses fundamentals and offers 34 designs. "Absolutely first rate . . . well thought out and well executed."–E. J. Tangerman. 118pp. 7¾ x 10⅝.
23654-4

ILLUSTRATED CATALOG OF CIVIL WAR MILITARY GOODS: Union Army Weapons, Insignia, Uniform Accessories, and Other Equipment, Schuyler, Hartley, and Graham. Rare, profusely illustrated 1846 catalog includes Union Army uniform and dress regulations, arms and ammunition, coats, insignia, flags, swords, rifles, etc. 226 illustrations. 160pp. 9 x 12.
24939-5

WOMEN'S FASHIONS OF THE EARLY 1900s: An Unabridged Republication of "New York Fashions, 1909," National Cloak & Suit Co. Rare catalog of mail-order fashions documents women's and children's clothing styles shortly after the turn of the century. Captions offer full descriptions, prices. Invaluable resource for fashion, costume historians. Approximately 725 illustrations. 128pp. 8⅜ x 11¼.
27276-1

THE 1912 AND 1915 GUSTAV STICKLEY FURNITURE CATALOGS, Gustav Stickley. With over 200 detailed illustrations and descriptions, these two catalogs are essential reading and reference materials and identification guides for Stickley furniture. Captions cite materials, dimensions and prices. 112pp. 6½ x 9¼.
26676-1

EARLY AMERICAN LOCOMOTIVES, John H. White, Jr. Finest locomotive engravings from early 19th century: historical (1804–74), main-line (after 1870), special, foreign, etc. 147 plates. 142pp. 11⅜ x 8¼.
22772-3

THE TALL SHIPS OF TODAY IN PHOTOGRAPHS, Frank O. Braynard. Lavishly illustrated tribute to nearly 100 majestic contemporary sailing vessels: Amerigo Vespucci, Clearwater, Constitution, Eagle, Mayflower, Sea Cloud, Victory, many more. Authoritative captions provide statistics, background on each ship. 190 black-and-white photographs and illustrations. Introduction. 128pp. 8⅞ x 11¾.
27163-3

CATALOG OF DOVER BOOKS

LITTLE BOOK OF EARLY AMERICAN CRAFTS AND TRADES, Peter Stockham (ed.). 1807 children's book explains crafts and trades: baker, hatter, cooper, potter, and many others. 23 copperplate illustrations. 140pp. 4⅝ x 6. 23336-7

VICTORIAN FASHIONS AND COSTUMES FROM HARPER'S BAZAR, 1867–1898, Stella Blum (ed.). Day costumes, evening wear, sports clothes, shoes, hats, other accessories in over 1,000 detailed engravings. 320pp. 9⅜ x 12¼. 22990-4

GUSTAV STICKLEY, THE CRAFTSMAN, Mary Ann Smith. Superb study surveys broad scope of Stickley's achievement, especially in architecture. Design philosophy, rise and fall of the Craftsman empire, descriptions and floor plans for many Craftsman houses, more. 86 black-and-white halftones. 31 line illustrations. Introduction 208pp. 6½ x 9¼. 27210-9

THE LONG ISLAND RAIL ROAD IN EARLY PHOTOGRAPHS, Ron Ziel. Over 220 rare photos, informative text document origin (1844) and development of rail service on Long Island. Vintage views of early trains, locomotives, stations, passengers, crews, much more. Captions. 8⅞ x 11¾. 26301-0

VOYAGE OF THE LIBERDADE, Joshua Slocum. Great 19th-century mariner's thrilling, first-hand account of the wreck of his ship off South America, the 35-foot boat he built from the wreckage, and its remarkable voyage home. 128pp. 5⅜ x 8½. 40022-0

TEN BOOKS ON ARCHITECTURE, Vitruvius. The most important book ever written on architecture. Early Roman aesthetics, technology, classical orders, site selection, all other aspects. Morgan translation. 331pp. 5⅜ x 8½. 20645-9

THE HUMAN FIGURE IN MOTION, Eadweard Muybridge. More than 4,500 stopped-action photos, in action series, showing undraped men, women, children jumping, lying down, throwing, sitting, wrestling, carrying, etc. 390pp. 7⅞ x 10⅝. 20204-6 Clothbd.

TREES OF THE EASTERN AND CENTRAL UNITED STATES AND CANADA, William M. Harlow. Best one-volume guide to 140 trees. Full descriptions, woodlore, range, etc. Over 600 illustrations. Handy size. 288pp. 4½ x 6⅜. 20395-6

SONGS OF WESTERN BIRDS, Dr. Donald J. Borror. Complete song and call repertoire of 60 western species, including flycatchers, juncoes, cactus wrens, many more–includes fully illustrated booklet. Cassette and manual 99913-0

GROWING AND USING HERBS AND SPICES, Milo Miloradovich. Versatile handbook provides all the information needed for cultivation and use of all the herbs and spices available in North America. 4 illustrations. Index. Glossary. 236pp. 5⅜ x 8½. 25058-X

BIG BOOK OF MAZES AND LABYRINTHS, Walter Shepherd. 50 mazes and labyrinths in all–classical, solid, ripple, and more–in one great volume. Perfect inexpensive puzzler for clever youngsters. Full solutions. 112pp. 8⅛ x 11. 22951-3

CATALOG OF DOVER BOOKS

PIANO TUNING, J. Cree Fischer. Clearest, best book for beginner, amateur. Simple repairs, raising dropped notes, tuning by easy method of flattened fifths. No previous skills needed. 4 illustrations. 201pp. 5⅜ x 8½. 23267-0

HINTS TO SINGERS, Lillian Nordica. Selecting the right teacher, developing confidence, overcoming stage fright, and many other important skills receive thoughtful discussion in this indispensible guide, written by a world-famous diva of four decades' experience. 96pp. 5⅜ x 8½. 40094-8

THE COMPLETE NONSENSE OF EDWARD LEAR, Edward Lear. All nonsense limericks, zany alphabets, Owl and Pussycat, songs, nonsense botany, etc., illustrated by Lear. Total of 320pp. 5⅜ x 8½. (Available in U.S. only.) 20167-8

VICTORIAN PARLOUR POETRY: An Annotated Anthology, Michael R. Turner. 117 gems by Longfellow, Tennyson, Browning, many lesser-known poets. "The Village Blacksmith," "Curfew Must Not Ring Tonight," "Only a Baby Small," dozens more, often difficult to find elsewhere. Index of poets, titles, first lines. xxiii + 325pp. 5⅜ x 8¼. 27044-0

DUBLINERS, James Joyce. Fifteen stories offer vivid, tightly focused observations of the lives of Dublin's poorer classes. At least one, "The Dead," is considered a masterpiece. Reprinted complete and unabridged from standard edition. 160pp. 5³⁄₁₆ x 8¼. 26870-5

GREAT WEIRD TALES: 14 Stories by Lovecraft, Blackwood, Machen and Others, S. T. Joshi (ed.). 14 spellbinding tales, including "The Sin Eater," by Fiona McLeod, "The Eye Above the Mantel," by Frank Belknap Long, as well as renowned works by R. H. Barlow, Lord Dunsany, Arthur Machen, W. C. Morrow and eight other masters of the genre. 256pp. 5⅜ x 8½. (Available in U.S. only.) 40436-6

THE BOOK OF THE SACRED MAGIC OF ABRAMELIN THE MAGE, translated by S. MacGregor Mathers. Medieval manuscript of ceremonial magic. Basic document in Aleister Crowley, Golden Dawn groups. 268pp. 5⅜ x 8½. 23211-5

NEW RUSSIAN-ENGLISH AND ENGLISH-RUSSIAN DICTIONARY, M. A. O'Brien. This is a remarkably handy Russian dictionary, containing a surprising amount of information, including over 70,000 entries. 366pp. 4½ x 6⅛. 20208-9

HISTORIC HOMES OF THE AMERICAN PRESIDENTS, Second, Revised Edition, Irvin Haas. A traveler's guide to American Presidential homes, most open to the public, depicting and describing homes occupied by every American President from George Washington to George Bush. With visiting hours, admission charges, travel routes. 175 photographs. Index. 160pp. 8¼ x 11. 26751-2

NEW YORK IN THE FORTIES, Andreas Feininger. 162 brilliant photographs by the well-known photographer, formerly with *Life* magazine. Commuters, shoppers, Times Square at night, much else from city at its peak. Captions by John von Hartz. 181pp. 9¼ x 10¾. 23585-8

INDIAN SIGN LANGUAGE, William Tomkins. Over 525 signs developed by Sioux and other tribes. Written instructions and diagrams. Also 290 pictographs. 111pp. 6⅛ x 9¼. 22029-X

ANATOMY: A Complete Guide for Artists, Joseph Sheppard. A master of figure drawing shows artists how to render human anatomy convincingly. Over 460 illustrations. 224pp. 8⅜ x 11¼. 27279-6

MEDIEVAL CALLIGRAPHY: Its History and Technique, Marc Drogin. Spirited history, comprehensive instruction manual covers 13 styles (ca. 4th century through 15th). Excellent photographs; directions for duplicating medieval techniques with modern tools. 224pp. 8⅜ x 11¼. 26142-5

DRIED FLOWERS: How to Prepare Them, Sarah Whitlock and Martha Rankin. Complete instructions on how to use silica gel, meal and borax, perlite aggregate, sand and borax, glycerine and water to create attractive permanent flower arrangements. 12 illustrations. 32pp. 5⅜ x 8½. 21802-3

EASY-TO-MAKE BIRD FEEDERS FOR WOODWORKERS, Scott D. Campbell. Detailed, simple-to-use guide for designing, constructing, caring for and using feeders. Text, illustrations for 12 classic and contemporary designs. 96pp. 5⅜ x 8½. 25847-5

SCOTTISH WONDER TALES FROM MYTH AND LEGEND, Donald A. Mackenzie. 16 lively tales tell of giants rumbling down mountainsides, of a magic wand that turns stone pillars into warriors, of gods and goddesses, evil hags, powerful forces and more. 240pp. 5⅜ x 8½. 29677-6

THE HISTORY OF UNDERCLOTHES, C. Willett Cunnington and Phyllis Cunnington. Fascinating, well-documented survey covering six centuries of English undergarments, enhanced with over 100 illustrations: 12th-century laced-up bodice, footed long drawers (1795), 19th-century bustles, 19th-century corsets for men, Victorian "bust improvers," much more. 272pp. 5⅝ x 8¼. 27124-2

ARTS AND CRAFTS FURNITURE: The Complete Brooks Catalog of 1912, Brooks Manufacturing Co. Photos and detailed descriptions of more than 150 now very collectible furniture designs from the Arts and Crafts movement depict davenports, settees, buffets, desks, tables, chairs, bedsteads, dressers and more, all built of solid, quarter-sawed oak. Invaluable for students and enthusiasts of antiques, Americana and the decorative arts. 80pp. 6½ x 9¼. 27471-3

WILBUR AND ORVILLE: A Biography of the Wright Brothers, Fred Howard. Definitive, crisply written study tells the full story of the brothers' lives and work. A vividly written biography, unparalleled in scope and color, that also captures the spirit of an extraordinary era. 560pp. 6⅛ x 9¼. 40297-5

THE ARTS OF THE SAILOR: Knotting, Splicing and Ropework, Hervey Garrett Smith. Indispensable shipboard reference covers tools, basic knots and useful hitches; handsewing and canvas work, more. Over 100 illustrations. Delightful reading for sea lovers. 256pp. 5⅜ x 8½. 26440-8

FRANK LLOYD WRIGHT'S FALLINGWATER: The House and Its History, Second, Revised Edition, Donald Hoffmann. A total revision–both in text and illustrations–of the standard document on Fallingwater, the boldest, most personal architectural statement of Wright's mature years, updated with valuable new material from the recently opened Frank Lloyd Wright Archives. "Fascinating"–*The New York Times.* 116 illustrations. 128pp. 9¼ x 10¾. 27430-6

CATALOG OF DOVER BOOKS

PHOTOGRAPHIC SKETCHBOOK OF THE CIVIL WAR, Alexander Gardner. 100 photos taken on field during the Civil War. Famous shots of Manassas Harper's Ferry, Lincoln, Richmond, slave pens, etc. 244pp. 10⅝ x 8¼. 22731-6

FIVE ACRES AND INDEPENDENCE, Maurice G. Kains. Great back-to-the-land classic explains basics of self-sufficient farming. The one book to get. 95 illustrations. 397pp. 5⅜ x 8½. 20974-1

SONGS OF EASTERN BIRDS, Dr. Donald J. Borror. Songs and calls of 60 species most common to eastern U.S.: warblers, woodpeckers, flycatchers, thrushes, larks, many more in high-quality recording. Cassette and manual 99912-2

A MODERN HERBAL, Margaret Grieve. Much the fullest, most exact, most useful compilation of herbal material. Gigantic alphabetical encyclopedia, from aconite to zedoary, gives botanical information, medical properties, folklore, economic uses, much else. Indispensable to serious reader. 161 illustrations. 888pp. 6½ x 9¼. 2-vol. set. (Available in U.S. only.) Vol. I: 22798-7
Vol. II: 22799-5

HIDDEN TREASURE MAZE BOOK, Dave Phillips. Solve 34 challenging mazes accompanied by heroic tales of adventure. Evil dragons, people-eating plants, blood-thirsty giants, many more dangerous adversaries lurk at every twist and turn. 34 mazes, stories, solutions. 48pp. 8¼ x 11. 24566-7

LETTERS OF W. A. MOZART, Wolfgang A. Mozart. Remarkable letters show bawdy wit, humor, imagination, musical insights, contemporary musical world; includes some letters from Leopold Mozart. 276pp. 5⅜ x 8½. 22859-2

BASIC PRINCIPLES OF CLASSICAL BALLET, Agrippina Vaganova. Great Russian theoretician, teacher explains methods for teaching classical ballet. 118 illustrations. 175pp. 5⅜ x 8½. 22036-2

THE JUMPING FROG, Mark Twain. Revenge edition. The original story of The Celebrated Jumping Frog of Calaveras County, a hapless French translation, and Twain's hilarious "retranslation" from the French. 12 illustrations. 66pp. 5⅜ x 8½. 22686-7

BEST REMEMBERED POEMS, Martin Gardner (ed.). The 126 poems in this superb collection of 19th- and 20th-century British and American verse range from Shelley's "To a Skylark" to the impassioned "Renascence" of Edna St. Vincent Millay and to Edward Lear's whimsical "The Owl and the Pussycat." 224pp. 5⅜ x 8½. 27165-X

COMPLETE SONNETS, William Shakespeare. Over 150 exquisite poems deal with love, friendship, the tyranny of time, beauty's evanescence, death and other themes in language of remarkable power, precision and beauty. Glossary of archaic terms. 80pp. 5³⁄₁₆ x 8¼. 26686-9

THE BATTLES THAT CHANGED HISTORY, Fletcher Pratt. Eminent historian profiles 16 crucial conflicts, ancient to modern, that changed the course of civilization. 352pp. 5⅜ x 8½. 41129-X

THE WIT AND HUMOR OF OSCAR WILDE, Alvin Redman (ed.). More than 1,000 ripostes, paradoxes, wisecracks: Work is the curse of the drinking classes; I can resist everything except temptation; etc. 258pp. 5⅜ x 8½. 20602-5

SHAKESPEARE LEXICON AND QUOTATION DICTIONARY, Alexander Schmidt. Full definitions, locations, shades of meaning in every word in plays and poems. More than 50,000 exact quotations. 1,485pp. 6½ x 9¼. 2-vol. set.
Vol. 1: 22726-X
Vol. 2: 22727-8

SELECTED POEMS, Emily Dickinson. Over 100 best-known, best-loved poems by one of America's foremost poets, reprinted from authoritative early editions. No comparable edition at this price. Index of first lines. 64pp. 5³⁄₁₆ x 8¼. 26466-1

THE INSIDIOUS DR. FU-MANCHU, Sax Rohmer. The first of the popular mystery series introduces a pair of English detectives to their archnemesis, the diabolical Dr. Fu-Manchu. Flavorful atmosphere, fast-paced action, and colorful characters enliven this classic of the genre. 208pp. 5³⁄₁₆ x 8¼. 29898-1

THE MALLEUS MALEFICARUM OF KRAMER AND SPRENGER, translated by Montague Summers. Full text of most important witchhunter's "bible," used by both Catholics and Protestants. 278pp. 6⅝ x 10. 22802-9

SPANISH STORIES/CUENTOS ESPAÑOLES: A Dual-Language Book, Angel Flores (ed.). Unique format offers 13 great stories in Spanish by Cervantes, Borges, others. Faithful English translations on facing pages. 352pp. 5⅜ x 8½. 25399-6

GARDEN CITY, LONG ISLAND, IN EARLY PHOTOGRAPHS, 1869–1919, Mildred H. Smith. Handsome treasury of 118 vintage pictures, accompanied by carefully researched captions, document the Garden City Hotel fire (1899), the Vanderbilt Cup Race (1908), the first airmail flight departing from the Nassau Boulevard Aerodrome (1911), and much more. 96pp. 8⅞ x 11¾. 40669-5

OLD QUEENS, N.Y., IN EARLY PHOTOGRAPHS, Vincent F. Seyfried and William Asadorian. Over 160 rare photographs of Maspeth, Jamaica, Jackson Heights, and other areas. Vintage views of DeWitt Clinton mansion, 1939 World's Fair and more. Captions. 192pp. 8⅞ x 11. 26358-4

CAPTURED BY THE INDIANS: 15 Firsthand Accounts, 1750-1870, Frederick Drimmer. Astounding true historical accounts of grisly torture, bloody conflicts, relentless pursuits, miraculous escapes and more, by people who lived to tell the tale. 384pp. 5⅜ x 8½. 24901-8

THE WORLD'S GREAT SPEECHES (Fourth Enlarged Edition), Lewis Copeland, Lawrence W. Lamm, and Stephen J. McKenna. Nearly 300 speeches provide public speakers with a wealth of updated quotes and inspiration–from Pericles' funeral oration and William Jennings Bryan's "Cross of Gold Speech" to Malcolm X's powerful words on the Black Revolution and Earl of Spenser's tribute to his sister, Diana, Princess of Wales. 944pp. 5⅜ x 8⅜. 40903-1

THE BOOK OF THE SWORD, Sir Richard F. Burton. Great Victorian scholar/adventurer's eloquent, erudite history of the "queen of weapons"–from prehistory to early Roman Empire. Evolution and development of early swords, variations (sabre, broadsword, cutlass, scimitar, etc.), much more. 336pp. 6⅛ x 9¼. 25434-8

AUTOBIOGRAPHY: The Story of My Experiments with Truth, Mohandas K. Gandhi. Boyhood, legal studies, purification, the growth of the Satyagraha (nonviolent protest) movement. Critical, inspiring work of the man responsible for the freedom of India. 480pp. 5⅜ x 8½. (Available in U.S. only.) 24593-4

CELTIC MYTHS AND LEGENDS, T. W. Rolleston. Masterful retelling of Irish and Welsh stories and tales. Cuchulain, King Arthur, Deirdre, the Grail, many more. First paperback edition. 58 full-page illustrations. 512pp. 5⅜ x 8½. 26507-2

THE PRINCIPLES OF PSYCHOLOGY, William James. Famous long course complete, unabridged. Stream of thought, time perception, memory, experimental methods; great work decades ahead of its time. 94 figures. 1,391pp. 5⅜ x 8½. 2-vol. set. Vol. I: 20381-6 Vol. II: 20382-4

THE WORLD AS WILL AND REPRESENTATION, Arthur Schopenhauer. Definitive English translation of Schopenhauer's life work, correcting more than 1,000 errors, omissions in earlier translations. Translated by E. F. J. Payne. Total of 1,269pp. 5⅜ x 8½. 2-vol. set. Vol. 1: 21761-2 Vol. 2: 21762-0

MAGIC AND MYSTERY IN TIBET, Madame Alexandra David-Neel. Experiences among lamas, magicians, sages, sorcerers, Bonpa wizards. A true psychic discovery. 32 illustrations. 321pp. 5⅜ x 8½. (Available in U.S. only.) 22682-4

THE EGYPTIAN BOOK OF THE DEAD, E. A. Wallis Budge. Complete reproduction of Ani's papyrus, finest ever found. Full hieroglyphic text, interlinear transliteration, word-for-word translation, smooth translation. 533pp. 6½ x 9¼. 21866-X

MATHEMATICS FOR THE NONMATHEMATICIAN, Morris Kline. Detailed, college-level treatment of mathematics in cultural and historical context, with numerous exercises. Recommended Reading Lists. Tables. Numerous figures. 641pp. 5⅜ x 8½. 24823-2

PROBABILISTIC METHODS IN THE THEORY OF STRUCTURES, Isaac Elishakoff. Well-written introduction covers the elements of the theory of probability from two or more random variables, the reliability of such multivariable structures, the theory of random function, Monte Carlo methods of treating problems incapable of exact solution, and more. Examples. 502pp. 5⅜ x 8½. 40691-1

THE RIME OF THE ANCIENT MARINER, Gustave Doré, S. T. Coleridge. Doré's finest work; 34 plates capture moods, subtleties of poem. Flawless full-size reproductions printed on facing pages with authoritative text of poem. "Beautiful. Simply beautiful."–*Publisher's Weekly*. 77pp. 9¼ x 12. 22305-1

NORTH AMERICAN INDIAN DESIGNS FOR ARTISTS AND CRAFTSPEOPLE, Eva Wilson. Over 360 authentic copyright-free designs adapted from Navajo blankets, Hopi pottery, Sioux buffalo hides, more. Geometrics, symbolic figures, plant and animal motifs, etc. 128pp. 8⅜ x 11. (Not for sale in the United Kingdom.) 25341-4

SCULPTURE: Principles and Practice, Louis Slobodkin. Step-by-step approach to clay, plaster, metals, stone; classical and modern. 253 drawings, photos. 255pp. 8⅛ x 11. 22960-2

THE INFLUENCE OF SEA POWER UPON HISTORY, 1660–1783, A. T. Mahan. Influential classic of naval history and tactics still used as text in war colleges. First paperback edition. 4 maps. 24 battle plans. 640pp. 5⅜ x 8½. 25509-3

CATALOG OF DOVER BOOKS

THE STORY OF THE TITANIC AS TOLD BY ITS SURVIVORS, Jack Winocour (ed.). What it was really like. Panic, despair, shocking inefficiency, and a little heroism. More thrilling than any fictional account. 26 illustrations. 320pp. 5⅜ x 8½.
20610-6

FAIRY AND FOLK TALES OF THE IRISH PEASANTRY, William Butler Yeats (ed.). Treasury of 64 tales from the twilight world of Celtic myth and legend: "The Soul Cages," "The Kildare Pooka," "King O'Toole and his Goose," many more. Introduction and Notes by W. B. Yeats. 352pp. 5⅜ x 8½. 26941-8

BUDDHIST MAHAYANA TEXTS, E. B. Cowell and others (eds.). Superb, accurate translations of basic documents in Mahayana Buddhism, highly important in history of religions. The Buddha-karita of Asvaghosha, Larger Sukhavativyuha, more. 448pp. 5⅜ x 8½. 25552-2

ONE TWO THREE . . . INFINITY: Facts and Speculations of Science, George Gamow. Great physicist's fascinating, readable overview of contemporary science: number theory, relativity, fourth dimension, entropy, genes, atomic structure, much more. 128 illustrations. Index. 352pp. 5⅜ x 8½. 25664-2

EXPERIMENTATION AND MEASUREMENT, W. J. Youden. Introductory manual explains laws of measurement in simple terms and offers tips for achieving accuracy and minimizing errors. Mathematics of measurement, use of instruments, experimenting with machines. 1994 edition. Foreword. Preface. Introduction. Epilogue. Selected Readings. Glossary. Index. Tables and figures. 128pp. 5⅜ x 8½. 40451-X

DALÍ ON MODERN ART: The Cuckolds of Antiquated Modern Art, Salvador Dalí. Influential painter skewers modern art and its practitioners. Outrageous evaluations of Picasso, Cézanne, Turner, more. 15 renderings of paintings discussed. 44 calligraphic decorations by Dalí. 96pp. 5⅜ x 8½. (Available in U.S. only.) 29220-7

ANTIQUE PLAYING CARDS: A Pictorial History, Henry René D'Allemagne. Over 900 elaborate, decorative images from rare playing cards (14th–20th centuries): Bacchus, death, dancing dogs, hunting scenes, royal coats of arms, players cheating, much more. 96pp. 9¼ x 12¼. 29265-7

MAKING FURNITURE MASTERPIECES: 30 Projects with Measured Drawings, Franklin H. Gottshall. Step-by-step instructions, illustrations for constructing handsome, useful pieces, among them a Sheraton desk, Chippendale chair, Spanish desk, Queen Anne table and a William and Mary dressing mirror. 224pp. 8⅛ x 11¼.
29338-6

THE FOSSIL BOOK: A Record of Prehistoric Life, Patricia V. Rich et al. Profusely illustrated definitive guide covers everything from single-celled organisms and dinosaurs to birds and mammals and the interplay between climate and man. Over 1,500 illustrations. 760pp. 7½ x 10⅛. 29371-8